PENGUIN BOOKS
Cnut

Ryan Lavelle is Professor in Early Medieval History at the University of Winchester and a leading expert on the history of Wessex. His books include *Alfred's Wars* and *Aethelred II: King of the English, 978–1016*.

T0006004

RYAN LAVELLE

Cnut

The North Sea King

PENGUIN BOOKS

PENGUIN BOOKS

UK | USA | Canada | Ireland | Australia
India | New Zealand | South Africa

Penguin Books is part of the Penguin Random House group of companies
whose addresses can be found at global.penguinrandomhouse.com

First published by Allen Lane 2017
Published in Penguin Books 2021
002

Typeset by Jouve (UK), Milton Keynes
Printed and bound in Great Britain by Clays Ltd, Elcograf S.p.A.

The authorized representative in the EEA is Penguin Random House Ireland,
Morrison Chambers, 32 Nassau Street, Dublin D02 YH68

ISBN: 978-0-141-99936-4

www.greenpenguin.co.uk

Contents

Note on the Text   ix
Maps   xiii
Genealogical Table   xv

CNUT

1. Cnut the Conqueror   3
2. King of the English   26
3. From England to Denmark   40
4. Wider Still, and Wider   55
5. Into Realms Beyond   67
6. The End of Danish England   83

Notes   89
Further Reading   101
Picture Credits   105
Acknowledgements   107
Index   109

For Benjamin

Note on the Text

NAMES AND SOURCES

Historical names can prove difficult in a book like this, which attempts to tread a fine line between accessibility and the complexities of early medieval societies. With names sometimes sounding odd and even alienating to the modern anglophone ear, how to render them in print can be the bane of editors and typesetters, not to mention authors. Although there are no tricky long-abandoned letters such as þ or ð to worry about, the choice of spelling is an issue when it comes to our protagonist, the self-styled 'King of all England and Denmark, and the Norwegians, and Part of the Swedes', whose name, meaning 'Knot' in Old Norse, can be rendered Knútr, Knud, Knut, Cnut or Canute. In some ways, the variety reflects the various identities and audiences of this ruler. Versions of the traditional anglophone rendering, 'Canute', were occasionally used in some Anglo-Latin documents and 'Canute' still crops up today in such diverse circumstances as the name of a street or of a transport company. Old Norse sources tend to run with variations of 'Knútr', while many modern Scandinavian historians use the modern personal name 'Knud' (Danish) or 'Knut' (Swedish and Norwegian, and also the name of a famous polar bear in Berlin Zoo). In England, the letter K was only stuttering into use in the eleventh century and 'Cnut' was used on coins and in many contemporary English documents, including the annals from the period known to us as the *Anglo-Saxon Chronicle*. As this is a book on an English king – or at least a 'King of England' – for a series about English monarchs it seems appropriate to make that choice here and refer to him as 'Cnut'.

The different ways in which Cnut was remembered reflects the range of sources for the period of his reign (1017–35). The *Anglo-Saxon Chronicle* provides a court-focused narrative of the main events of the Anglo-Saxon period in the contemporary vernacular of Old English. Despite recording events in year-by-year annals, the *Chronicle* for much of our period is likely to have been compiled by a single author (referred to here as the 'Chronicler'), between about 1017 and 1023, perhaps even in a single writing campaign that brought together the early years of Cnut's reign with those of his predecessors Æthelred 'the Unready' (978–1016) and Edmund 'Ironside' (1016). The Chronicler's criticisms of some of those who surrounded the kings of the time makes it difficult to determine whether the writer of the *Chronicle* favoured the advent of Cnut's reign. Whatever his thoughts, the Chronicler does not seem hostile to Cnut himself. Historians may supplement the words of the *Chronicle* with those of a Flemish author writing an encomium for Cnut's English queen, Emma, a few years after Cnut's death.[1] These narrative sources may draw on the memories of those who were around Cnut during his reign, but they should be used with care. The authors of the time were not writing with the aim of providing an accurate record for posterity and there is much that the *Chronicle* and the *Encomium Emmae Reginae* do not say. For a fuller picture of the king, we must draw from a wider range of records, from the intricately composed Old Norse of skalds, or court poets, through to the statements of Christian piety in Latin and Old English in charters and laws, as well as the few visual depictions of Cnut's kingship that survive: the images of his head hammered on coins in England and Scandinavia or the depiction of the king with Queen Emma in a Winchester monastery's *Liber Vitae* ('Book of Life').

Yet still we lack the full story at crucial moments of Cnut's life, and we can only surmise his whereabouts during certain periods. This is not an uncommon problem when writing about early medieval rulers, but to make up for quite substantial gaps in our knowledge of Cnut, historians have often turned to later accounts, such as those of the twelfth-century Anglo-Norman chroniclers John of Worcester, William of Malmesbury and Henry of Huntingdon, and the late twelfth-century Scandinavian authors writing in Latin, Saxo Grammaticus and Sven Aggeson in Denmark, and Theodoric the Monk in Norway, as well as the Old Norse 'Kings' Sagas', the most famous of which were written by the thirteenth-century Icelandic politician Snorri Sturluson.

The siren song of the details provided by accounts like these is seductive, particularly when trying to build a biographical picture of character. A particularly pertinent case is that of the Icelandic *Knytlinga Saga*, written in the mid thirteenth century, which relates that Cnut was hand-some despite his thin and 'slightly crooked' nose, and was not particularly intelligent, just like his father, Swein Fork-beard, and *his* father before him![2] That reflection of the intelligence of the king in a line of not-so-clever rulers might be revelatory if we were to rely upon it in an exam-ination of Cnut as a ruler. Was he feckless and was any success of his simply due to good fortune? There were cer-tainly points in the king's reign when he was favoured by circumstances beyond his control, but we should not let a writer who is likely to have been as removed from direct knowledge of events as we are today determine how we read the eleventh-century Cnut. The motif of describing appearance linked with personality had been the stock-in-trade of authors since Charlemagne's biographer Einhard resurrected the classical form of biographical writing in the ninth century, and hence should not be taken at face value. Historians also need to proceed with caution when picking their way through fragmentary sources. And, as we shall see below, this applies to the best-known, if apoc-ryphal, episode associated with Cnut.

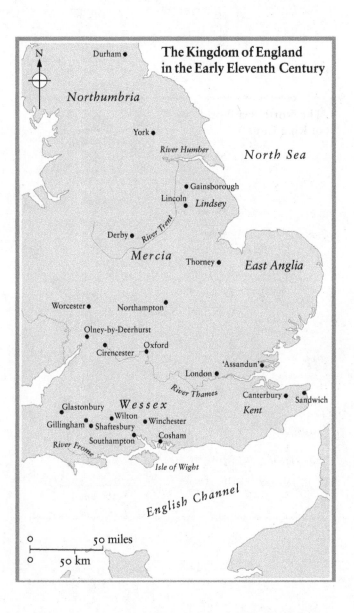

The Kingdom of England in the Early Eleventh Century

The North Sea World of King Cnut

Norwegian Sea

Lade
Stiklestad
Trøndelag

SWEDEN

NORWAY

Uppland

Shetland

Orkney
Pentland Firth
Caithness

Oslo Fjord

SCOTLAND

North Sea

DENMARK
Jelling

Holy River?

Skåne

Roskilde

Strathclyde

Dublin

York

Wolin

ENGLAND

London

Winchester

Ghent
Saint-Omer
Flanders

Channel Islands

Fécamp

Normandy

Mont-Saint-Michel

Chartres

N

0   300 miles
0   300 km

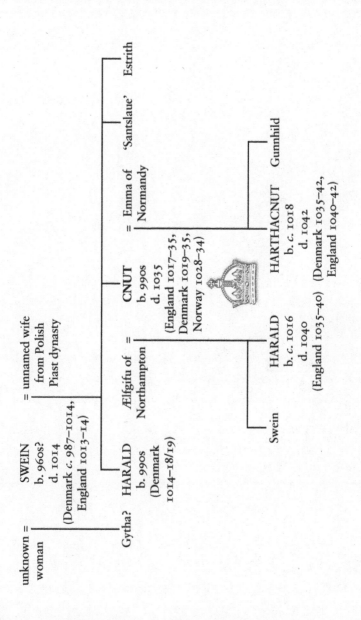

Cnut

I

Cnut the Conqueror

The words of the twelfth-century historian Henry of Huntingdon may have had the greatest impact on our view of Cnut today. At the height of his power, according to Henry, Cnut ordered his throne to be taken to the seashore 'as the tide was coming in'. The imperious nature of the king's command to the rising sea is famous in the traditional narratives of English history, even if the words themselves are less well known:

> You are subject to me, as the land on which I am sitting is mine, and no one has resisted my overlordship with impunity. I command you, therefore, not to rise on to my land, nor to presume to wet the clothing or limbs of your master.[1]

The command is normally read in terms of Cnut teaching a lesson to his fawning courtiers, but it is the king who is shown to learn his lesson. The tide does not do as Cnut commands and Henry has him declare that, compared with that of God, 'the power of kings is empty and worthless'.[2]

Popular memory is created through such myths. If we were to believe that Cnut really was so arrogant as to try to command the tide, we might recall with a wry smile the limited intelligence reported by the *Knytlinga Saga*. A more generous interpretation might be determined by the boundless ambition of the aspiring emperor finally held in check by the power of the natural world. However, the lesson for a ruler has more to do with Henry's view of Anglo-Norman politics than Anglo-Danish power and it is interesting that Henry used Cnut, a figure whose realm then stretched across seas, to inform Anglo-Norman monarchs whose realms likewise stretched across the English Channel. Cnut, a conqueror of kingdoms whose power had grown with his achievements, was an apt choice. He is less well remembered today than the conquerors who came after him and Henry of Huntingdon's vignette is now the only episode by which he is popularly known. A mighty ruler who once dominated the North Sea has been relegated to a bit part in the popular perception of medieval history. But we should bear in mind that the very fact that this episode was attributed to him at a time when historical writing was being revived shows the regard in which Cnut was held in twelfth-century England.[3] His reputation had been built on solid eleventh-century foundations.

There is a certain irony that later generations have been keen to link the failed attempt to stop the tide with their own location, whether Southampton, Bosham (West Sussex), where Victorian tradition associates a child's grave with a drowned daughter of Cnut, or even, following another twelfth-century telling of the story, the tidal creek at Westminster. This is all part of the creation of myth in popular history, but such elaborations on the legend reflect the way in which the sea and shore did form an important part of Cnut's power. Skalds reciting poems at Cnut's court, who were paid vast sums to extol the virtues of the king, returned again and again to the image of great fleets of ships.[4] This was no mere hyperbole. Cnut crossed the sea, particularly the North Sea, strikingly often throughout his reign. As we shall see, he travelled from the south of his new English kingdom to Denmark where he claimed his paternal kingdom, and from Denmark east to the Baltic where he projected Danish power in regional disputes in which his Polish mother's royal ancestry gave him a stake,[5] north to Sweden to protect his interests there, and to Norway to build an empire.

What is more, the discovery in 1997 of the longest Viking ship yet known, 'Roskilde 6', dated by its timbers to Cnut's reign, built of Norwegian wood and found at the heart of his Danish realm, gives a tangible sense of the means by which Cnut's power might have been exercised. It may even have been a royal flagship in which Cnut himself sailed.[6] (See picture 10 in the plate section.)

The seashore also provides the setting for the moment at which Cnut first became a political actor in English history. In contrast to Henry of Huntingdon's tale of a tidal washout, we can be confident that the event in question actually happened. The setting is Sandwich, Kent, in the spring months of 1014. The young Dane, not yet a king, was with his fleet when an order was given for the hands, ears and noses of the English hostages in his charge to be cut off. The mutilation of the hostages' genitals is a detail added later by Norman writers,[7] but the *Anglo-Saxon Chronicle*, a reasonably contemporary record, provides enough information for us to know that this was a dramatic event in Cnut's history for which he was responsible.

Did this act take place on shore or on a ship, in view of locals or out of sight? Did Cnut himself step ashore? Did he take part in any of the bloodletting? Little further is known. The *Chronicle* implies that Cnut was the agent of the action himself, but at this time a leader need only give an order to take credit for what his men did in his name. The episode raises other questions that cannot be answered. Were the dismembered body parts displayed (the notion is not so odd for an age in which heads might be impaled on stakes) or were they simply cast into the sea? Were Cnut's actions intended as an extreme demonstration of his potential for political violence or as a Christian statement of imperial rule: making the hostages pay with their bodies for the sins of others while ensuring their souls were saved?[8] In the political maelstroms of the early Middle Ages, either would have been possible and neither explanation rules out the other, but whatever motivated him, Cnut, the young Prince of Denmark, had clearly made an impact, both literally and symbolically, on the lives of the English nobility.

These unfortunate hostages – now freed but disfigured – were not just sons of the men of Kent but had been living guarantees provided by the leading nobility from across England who had submitted to Cnut's father, Swein Fork-beard, as he became King of the English during the preceding year. We can be reasonably confident that the hostages were indeed men, and most probably young men, as hostageship was often a filial duty. One man, a certain Æthelwine, who had been 'deprived of his hands' while held hostage by the Danes, is recorded in a Worcestershire charter collection as a party in a property dispute a generation or so after Cnut's accession to the throne.[9] Although we cannot be certain that Æthelwine had been one of the actual hostages of 1014, his survival and evident importance in his community show that Cnut's action would have been intended as a permanent reminder to those who had provided the hostages.

The year 1014 has been given a grisly benchmark by the recent discovery in Dorset of the decapitated bodies of fifty or so likely Vikings, executed at some point in the later tenth or early eleventh century (probably before 1014). That act was evidently public, in a place linked with public authority.[10] Seen alongside that mass execution, Cnut's hostages may have felt lucky to have escaped with their lives, but Cnut may have been less concerned with killing than with broadcasting his dissatisfaction and demonstrating his determination to succeed as a political actor in England. He evidently intended to make his mark at the time in a way that would be remembered for some time thereafter.

In order to understand why Cnut should arrive at Sandwich and then depart, having left a hitherto-valuable bunch of hostages bleeding on the beach, we must look to the context of the struggle for the English kingdom in the reign of Æthelred the Unready, ruler since 978, and the waves of Viking attacks that had swept the kingdom since the 980s. These attacks were intensifying in the early eleventh century, requiring ever higher taxes to pay for military defences to repulse the Vikings or simply to pay them off. This gave rise to serious fractures among the English nobility. The Viking invasions help us to understand why the kingdom should have been under such pressure as to have accepted the invading Viking Swein Forkbeard as king, why Æthelred looked to Thorkell 'the Tall', a Danish warlord often at odds with Swein and later with Cnut, to provide a mercenary service to the English kingdom, and why many of the English nobility were eventually willing to accept Cnut as their king.

Cnut's father Swein Forkbeard, king in Denmark since the 980s, was scion of a dynasty that had been in control of a substantial Danish territory since the middle of the tenth century, only a little less time than England had been ruled (since the 920s) by Æthelred's branch of the English dynasty. We know next to nothing about Cnut's early life at this time, though Swein's father was Harald 'Bluetooth' (d. c. 987), during whose reign a number of monuments were erected across the Jutland peninsula, including a runestone at Jelling that proclaimed his rule over Denmark and Norway, boasting that he 'made the Danes Christian' (see picture 9),[11] and from which the dynasty is sometimes called the Jelling dynasty. Harald was the name of Swein's other known son, who became King of Denmark following Swein's death, so, given that this name was evidently a tribute to Swein's father, we might suppose that Cnut was younger than his brother (although the *Encomium* says just the opposite[12]). Cnut also had a half-sister, probably called Gytha, by a relationship that was evidently history long before he was born, and Cnut's mother, sister of a Polish king, was formerly married to a Swedish king until his death around 995,[13] so we can at least surmise that Cnut was not particularly old in 1014, probably not much older than the hostages he ordered to be mutilated. In a formal praise poem, a *drápa*, from later in Cnut's reign, the eleventh-century skaldic poet Ottar the Black reminded his audience that 'no younger prince ever departed his homeland'.[14] Given that skalds such as Ottar always flattered their patrons, Cnut's youth presumably mattered in the commemoration of conquest, and his actions were all the more remarkable for being a young leader in charge of a Viking fleet.

We have not seen the last of Cnut's family, but an important issue should be noted here. Although medieval chroniclers from the late eleventh century onwards portray Swein Fork-beard, accompanied by pagan followers, rebelling against his father Harald Bluetooth in the late tenth century, and while some modern commentators have followed this narrative, the evidence seems to be that though Swein probably did fight his father, who claimed to have made Denmark Christian, he was brought up a Christian and remained one.[15] Swein and his son Cnut, for all their 'Viking' interests in acquiring wealth and territory, were more than Viking warlords. They were Christian princes like many of their contemporaries across tenth- and eleventh-century Europe.

In eleventh-century England there was no problem in recognizing the authority of a Danish Christian king. The *Liber Vitae* of the monastic community at Durham records one '*Suain rex*' in its list of 'kings and dukes'.[16] While the twelfth-century scribe of that particular passage did not get Swein's place in the running order of rulers quite right, the point is that at Durham his memory was kept alive in the same way that it was for other Scots and English kings who mattered to that northern community. The Anglo-Saxon Chronicler relates Swein's rule to his receipt of submission from the northerners at Gainsborough (Lincolnshire) and the submission of southern nobles soon after, noting that King Æthelred went into exile, to Normandy via the Isle of Wight.[17] Swein still lacked formal consecration, a moment that would never come, but the fact that Swein had been accepted as king was important to his contemporaries.

Given that Swein had received the submission of many of the English nobility, it made sense for his son to marry into one of the groups that was most likely to provide more than nominal support. Ælfgifu of Northampton, Cnut's first wife, was the daughter of a nobleman murdered in a palace intrigue in 1006, the same year in which one of her brothers had been blinded and another murdered. Her family still remained powerful, though, with a large landed power base and much influence in the Midlands and the north of England.[18]

Again, the myths cloud our picture of Cnut. Because he later married Queen Emma (confusingly also known in England as Ælfgifu), the widow of his predecessor King Æthelred, and because the legitimacy of Cnut and Emma's marriage is emphasized by various sources, including one commissioned by Emma herself, the aforementioned *Encomium*, many have tended to follow that trail. This has meant playing down Cnut's relationship with Ælfgifu of Northampton, which continued throughout his reign. Historians have rationalized Cnut's marriage to Ælfgifu as being one 'in the Danish fashion' (*more Danico*), thus reading it as less meaningful, more 'pagan' even, than Christian marriage.[19] Such a reading is misleading. Ælfgifu was not Cnut's mistress of the sort that churchmen in later ages of reform might turn a blind eye to if circumstances suited. Cnut had married Ælfgifu. This meant that, when he later wed Emma, he would be married to two wives at the same time (albeit most likely they would have been living in different places), and contemporaries would have considered Cnut's marriage to Ælfgifu to have been as legitimate as his marriage to Emma.

Of course, marriage to a queen was in the future, and when Cnut married his first wife he was not king. But he would take a step closer to kingship in February 1014 when his father died, probably at Gainsborough, his seat of power. Death seems to have come suddenly. Emma's encomiast says that Swein had time to put his affairs in order, but it suited Emma's purposes to show that Cnut's legitimacy as the successor of his father was not in doubt.[20] Had Swein really had time to put his affairs in order he would have ensured that the English nobility swore to accept Cnut as his successor. As events transpired, Swein clearly did not. Later East Anglian tradition has Swein transfixed by a spear held by the dead royal saint, Edmund.[21] If we can perceive any record of Swein's actual death in this late eleventh-century transmission, a medical emergency might be represented in the form of a supernatural apparition. Saint Edmund's holy resistance against Vikings in the ninth century was preached during the reign of Æthelred,[22] and so it is not surprising that he should be linked with stories of Swein's sudden death.

What mattered to Cnut and Æthelred in the wake of Swein's death, and probably *really* mattered in the fate of the mutilated hostages, was that the English nobility decided that they were better off with the old king, Æthelred, rather than relying on the son of the Danish usurper with no other links to the English throne. A new Bishop of London was elected at an assembly in York just days after Swein's death, suggesting that the process of assembling a council (the Old English 'witan') in the North was already under way before the king died. Swein himself must therefore have called that witan, which Wulfstan, the politically astute Archbishop of York, had then overseen. So the first and last formal political act of the dead king was, inadvertently, to set in train the process that caused his predecessor to be recalled from his Norman exile.[23] Æthelred was sent for and on his return, as the *Anglo-Saxon Chronicle* tells us, using language indicative of a legal declaration, the king promised to be a good lord, to treat his nobility properly, mainly by avoiding hitting them with the sort of heavy taxes he had imposed in the past; in return, the nobility promised to support their 'natural lord'.[24] The *Chronicle*'s language at this point may reflect that the king's declaration had been drafted by Wulfstan, a figure who would later lend his support to Cnut but whose political agenda was served in 1014 by emphasizing that the English people were being punished for their desertion of God-given lordship, a message preached again and again – even after Cnut's accession to power – in Wulfstan's 'Sermon of the Wolf to the English'.[25]

Thus the story of Cnut as a political player in England is framed by the old king's return and what is recognized as the 'second reign' of Æthelred. Had the nobility gambled that Cnut, as the guardian of English hostages, would spare the lives and limbs of the young men given to Swein a year or so before? Swein's agreement with the English nobility probably died with him in February 1014, but Cnut would still have expected to be supported by the English nobles when he was declared king soon after Swein's death by the men of the Viking fleet. Although the rules of succession in England were not yet established, a close family member would normally succeed a ruling king.[26] Cnut must have hoped to build on the support that his marriage to Ælfgifu gave him from the Midland nobility, and the fact that he spent two months in England after Æthelred's return suggests that this support was not insubstantial. It was probably not enough, however, and the hostages he held did not provide him with the political leverage he needed. The *Anglo-Saxon Chronicle* records that Cnut was ambushed while gathering men and horses from the region of Lindsey, around Gainsborough, his father's power base, so he departed hastily. Despite his royal title, Cnut's foray into English affairs looked as though it was over before it had really begun.

As the *Chronicle* indicates, a quick move by a resurgent King Æthelred around April of that year meant that the 'wretched' people of Lindsey paid dearly for failing to reconnect with their southern-based king, perhaps being singled out for extreme violence because while other areas had also supported Swein, the region of Lindsey had retained allegiance with Cnut after Æthelred's return. Wreaking the divinely ordained vengeance of a wronged king, Æthelred and his men ravaged the lands just south of the Humber, killing all those 'who could be reached',[27] while Cnut made his departure for Denmark, only pausing, as we have seen, to send a grim message via his English hostages.

English politics continued to tumble through a messy course of events, but we hear few echoes of Cnut's activities in the interim until his return to England in 1015, when he made landfall at Sandwich once again. The *Encomium* notes that he had gone to Denmark and from this account we may discern the influence of another Viking warlord, Thorkell the Tall. Later Scandinavian tradition presents Thorkell as Cnut's foster-father, but this seems rather too simple an explanation for an important relationship, particularly given the contemporary detail that the two men later entrusted the care of their own sons to each other as part of a political deal. Thorkell's independence as 'jarl' (earl) of a dynasty in eastern Denmark that had once been kings was what really counted. Assertion of that independence was something that Cnut and, before him, Swein Forkbeard had to deal with.[28] Here the Encomiast's wish to stress Danish unity comes unstuck. He writes that while Thorkell had taken service with the English, it was not out of hostility towards Cnut, and that Thorkell even sought Cnut's favour by travelling to Denmark to see him.[29] Implying there were no hard feelings was evidently the best way of explaining away the forty-five ships of Thorkell's fleet that had defended Æthelred and London throughout much of 1013 in return for a large payment the previous year. We can't be certain whether Thorkell really left England for Denmark, but he seems to have been far from making an alliance with Cnut in 1014–15. A promise of £21,000 had been crucial in securing the continued service of Thorkell and his men for Æthelred on his return in

1014.[30] Cnut had probably tried and failed to secure the war-lord's aid when he travelled south along the English coast that year. At the very least, the presence of another Viking fleet in the service of the newly restored King Æthelred must have featured in Cnut's calculations when he landed in Sandwich before heading home.

Cnut's options may have been limited by the fact that his brother Harald was now king in Denmark, having succeeded their father Swein in 1014. Although there is some suggestion that the brothers shared power,[31] Harald's probable seniority may have limited what Cnut could do there, particularly if Thorkell retained controlling interests in the eastern part of the kingdom. It is unlikely that Harald came to England, as the German chronicler Thietmar of Merseburg states,[32] but Cnut does at least seem to have been more than just Thorkell and Harald's junior partner.

Though he may have been licking his wounds, Cnut had evidently not given up on England. Two prominent English thegns, Sigeferth and Morcar (possibly part of Cnut's wider family if he was then married to Ælfgifu), were killed in early 1015 and Æthelred's eldest surviving son, the ætheling Edmund (later known as Edmund 'Ironside'), was straining to exert his own influence. Heir to the throne and no doubt eager for more power, he launched a rebellion against his father, marrying Sigeferth's widow and claiming authority in the east Midlands.[33] If rumours of this upheaval reached Cnut, as is likely, it may have provided him with the opportunity he had been waiting for.

It is a hallmark of the maritime nature of Cnut's political world that he chose to return to Sandwich, where the

North Sea meets the English Channel (the 'South Sea', as it was also known). All was yet to play for. Sandwich itself *meant* something. It was the 'most famous' of English ports, in the view of the Encomiast, who mentioned few towns,[34] and it was where Æthelred had once gathered an immense fleet against Thorkell six years earlier, at a point before Thorkell was paid to defend the kingdom. That had been an episode which had gone horribly wrong for Æthelred as one of the English leaders took some ships from the fleet to pursue a vendetta against one of his rivals, giving the military advantage to Thorkell.[35] The port was quite a useful place for a Viking player to make his point, particularly as Viking fleets had also been there in the ninth century. As a strategically important site associated with political authority, the control of Sandwich was vital.

Despite the Midland focus of the upheaval going on in England in 1015, Cnut's campaign was, for the moment, directed towards taking Wessex, an area which, as the 'Kingdom of the West Saxons', was once ruled by Alfred the Great. Wessex was also, in many ways, still the heart of the English kingdom, where numerous royal lands and royally endowed churches lay. The *Anglo-Saxon Chronicle* reports that Cnut, who would have been with his fleet in the Channel, had 'turned at once round Kent into Wessex', to the mouth of the River Frome, landing in Dorset and ravaging there, as well as in Wiltshire and Somerset.[36] By comparison, Winchester and a good part of Wessex were evidently outside Cnut's immediate control. But, although still nominally king, Æthelred was not in control, either, perhaps because he then lay ill in the royal manor at Cosham, now a

suburb of Portsmouth, on the south coast. Æthelred probably had not meant to stay in England. He had gone into exile
once before and Portsmouth's later use as a point of departure by Anglo-Norman and Angevin kings gives us a clue
that Cosham, located on Portsmouth Harbour, may have
been intended as a place from which Æthelred could leave
his kingdom once again. The old king's place in Wessex and
England was evidently proving just as insecure under the
stresses of Cnut's activities in 1015 as had been the case during the activities of Cnut's father in 1013.

Æthelred's incapacity was evidently presenting Cnut
with an opportunity. By early 1016, Cnut may have felt
that the territory of Wessex was within his grasp. Indeed,
the *Anglo-Saxon Chronicle* records that the West Saxons
submitted to him. But at this crucial moment – perhaps the
West Saxons' submission had only been temporary – Cnut
seems to have diverted his attention northwards, first
through the Midlands and then to Northumbria. This was
a strategic error, though fortunately for him it was not a
fatal one and, seen through the prism of his experiences of
his father's rule, the decision was well founded. Swein Forkbeard had tasted English kingship through asserting his
authority in the North and East. Earl Uhtred of Northumbria, who had allied with the ætheling Edmund in 1016,
now came to submit to Cnut at or near York. Control of
Northumbria was a realistic aspiration for Cnut and was
perhaps his first, maybe even his only, strategic aim, possibly showing his first moves in Wessex as opportunistic.

The *Chronicle* goes on to say that Uhtred was subse-
quently murdered, an event given dramatic colour in a

Durham account.[37] If read as taking place immediately after Uhtred's submission, it seems a curious action at such a crucial point, though the principle of ordering the death of someone who no longer served his purpose does not seem out of character for Cnut. It is possible, however, that the Chronicler's phrase 'nevertheless he was killed'[38] was a later detail, added with hindsight – something quite common in this source. Uhtred may have continued to serve Cnut until after *c.* 1018, when Durham accounts associate him with the leadership of a Northumbrian army against a Scots–Strathclyde force and link the death of Uhtred with a later action undertaken by Cnut (at a time when Cnut was more secure).[39] Uhtred frustratingly remains a kind of eleventh-century Schrödinger's Cat, but, alive or dead in 1016, his relationship with Cnut reveals the future king's preoccupation with Northumbrian affairs at that point.

Cnut's northern actions may have given him the opportunity to develop his relationship with the master lawmaker and prelate, Wulfstan, Archbishop of York. Wulfstan's influence was important. Despite supporting the return of Æthelred in 1014, he had evidently given due honours in York to the body of Cnut's father, which may have remained there for some time prior to going to its final resting place in Denmark.[40] Cnut's relationship with Wulfstan would stand him in good stead in the years to come, but his momentary focus on Northumbria gave Æthelred's eldest surviving son Edmund the opportunity to come to his father, who had not crossed to Normandy, as many may have expected, but was now in London.[41] It is likely that Æthelred continued to be unwell as he had been unable to lead an English army against

Cnut at the start of 1016, but the crucial role of London in determining political affairs was now beginning to emerge.[42] As an increasingly important city, London *had* to be taken to secure the kingdom, and it was becoming the centre of resistance against Danish control. Cnut realized what was going on in the South and he did not need to settle for a merely northern kingdom. Returning from York, he ordered his troops to besiege London. The news that a fleet was on its way to the city may have hastened Æthelred's demise, perhaps from another bout of his earlier illnesses, and he passed away on Saint George's Day (23 April 1016).

Any ties of loyalty between the Viking warlord Thorkell and Æthelred must have died with the king, and it is perhaps telling that en route to London Cnut's fleet landed at Greenwich, where at least some of Thorkell's ships might still be found. Despite the Encomiast's attempts to show that Thorkell and Cnut had been on good terms when Cnut was in Denmark in 1014–15, it is not until April or May 1016, after Æthelred's death, that Thorkell is most likely to have made common cause with Cnut. Edmund escaped the city before Cnut's forces could reach it, but not before the citizens had accepted Edmund's kingship. The Viking strategy was a sound one, nevertheless. Throughout the campaigns that followed, the force surrounding the city evidently prevented Edmund from extending his kingship in Wessex to control of the city. Cnut never took London by siege or by storm and for a brief period Edmund managed to relieve the city and forced the Danes to retreat. However, the Danes quickly regrouped and the position of Cnut's forces outside the city determined that Cnut would come to control it once he and Edmund had finally made their peace agreement in October 1016.

Before that happened there were four months of hard campaigning while London was besieged by Cnut's forces and the first of the major battles took place at Penselwood, near the royal estate at Gillingham (Dorset), in June. Evidently England then had two rulers, even before Cnut and Edmund formally agreed to divide it after making peace. Indeed, John of Worcester, a twelfth-century writer who may have had access to earlier accounts, records that Cnut had received the submission of English nobles at Southampton *before* autumn 1016, promising in return to be a good lord.[43] John's account seems rather close in its wording to the declaration by Æthelred on his return in 1014, and reading this as a formal election to kingship, even a full coronation, is not impossible.[44]

Cnut evidently did not control all of the Vikings in England at that time, but as long as he could keep acquiring wealth he could still retain control of groups of warriors. Cnut's upper hand in the political situation may be indicated by what the coins of this period tell us – and what they do not. While coinage bearing Æthelred's name probably still circulated even after Cnut's eventual succession, if Cnut were accepted as king by some of the English during the summer of 1016, he could in principle issue coins as 'King of the English' prior to Edmund's death. As Cnut controlled a number of English towns, particularly those in the North, Midlands and East Anglia, it would make sense for his supporters, even for Cnut himself, to order coins to be issued proclaiming his dominance in those regions, and indeed some coins from the period bear his name.[45] A statement of kingship through the issuing of coins was typical of such struggles for power and in this light the simple absence of coins bearing Edmund's name is telling. The fact that Edmund was unable to assert his identity through coinage shows the extent to which Wessex was a contested zone for him rather than a place in which he might govern effectively.

Finally, a battle on 18 October 1016 proved decisive at a place in Essex called 'Assandun' (perhaps Ashingdon, Essex) by the Chronicler.[46] Although Edmund was not killed in the battle, one version of the *Anglo-Saxon Chronicle* includes the telling lament that 'all the nobility of England was destroyed there'.[47] The war of attrition had finally been won. The Chronicler blamed the English defeat on the treachery of a Mercian nobleman, Eadric 'Streona' ('Acquisitor'), who had risen to prominence during Æthelred's reign.[48] Prior to the battle, Eadric had apparently professed his loyalty to Edmund but his west Midland force fled early in the battle, an act portrayed in the *Chronicle* as a betrayal of King Edmund and 'all the people of England'.[49] Given that Edmund and Eadric were both dead by the time the *Chronicle* was composed, we might wonder whether there were other motivations. Eadric might just as easily have waited, like the Percys at the Battle of Bosworth (1485), before deciding on which side to fight. Eadric's reputation was low after his death in 1017, so transforming his role into that of an instigator of flight for the losing side may have been a convenient way of reminding Cnut's followers of the perils of failing to give their king wholehearted support.

The defining peace treaty was made in the autumn of 1016 at a place named by one locally connected contributor to the *Anglo-Saxon Chronicle* as 'Olney-by-Deerhurst'. Although the place name *Olan ige*, 'Ola's Island', is now lost, along with any knowledge of a real 'Ola', Deerhurst was an important site in Gloucestershire. Created by the waterlogging of the land around by tributaries of the River Severn, the island was a logical site for peacemaking. It lay between the southern territory of Wessex, where Edmund had established his power base, and the Midland territory of Mercia, suggesting that Edmund still had a position to negotiate from. Peace treaties were often made at island sites, and any rains of the autumn months would have served to heighten the sense of Olney's insularity.[50] The nearby minster church of Deerhurst may have been associated with the kindred of the ealdorman (governor) of the south-western provinces, Æthelmær, who had surrendered to Swein Forkbeard near Bath in 1013; Æthelmær seems to have been related to Odda, later ealdorman of the South-West, who would found a famous chapel at Deerhurst.[51] (See picture 8.)

Whether this is of any consequence in the choice of site is uncertain but Æthelmær's son was to die at Cnut's orders the following year, suggesting a connection between Æthelmær and Cnut. Twelfth-century writers naturally have much to say on such moments when personalities seem to emerge from the historical fog. Henry of Huntingdon associates the occasion with *actual* single combat between the two men. Although this is unlikely to have happened, that tradition was evidently already emerging in the eleventh century, as the *Encomium* reports an offer of single combat prior to the Battle of Assandun.[52] It may then have been a simple step to seeing Cnut and Edmund's encounter on an island as a *Holmgangr*, a Viking duel in a defined space.[53] Perhaps in Cnut's lifetime contemporaries were already thinking in those terms, particularly given the respect with which Edmund was evidently regarded as an opponent, but Old Norse tradition is full of such accounts, just as later Anglo-Norman accounts of battle begin with unaccepted offers of single combat. It was important enough that the two leaders met, talked and eventually divided the kingdom. Beneath the accretion of later story-telling, we might glimpse the reality of personality, a bond which seems to have developed between the two men, who were recorded by one version of the *Chronicle* as 'fellows and sworn brothers'.[54] Given their age and background, the bond may well have been genuine. There had, after all, been a hard summer of campaigning and in such circumstances, despite or perhaps because of the bloodshed, it was not impossible for the mutual respect of fellow warriors to develop into genuine affection. Though, as we will see, this would be a narrative that was to suit Cnut later in his reign, he would have had to have the memory of some relationship with Edmund for it to mean something to him.

Details of how the kingdom was divided are unknown. While the texts of a small handful of treaties survive from the Anglo-Saxon period, that of 1016 is not among them.[55] John of Worcester asserts that Edmund retained sovereignty over the kingdom as a whole. That may have been wishful thinking on John's part, based perhaps on an intention to project an unbroken English unity back into the tenth century, or simply a misreading of his source text.[56] Two *Anglo-Saxon Chronicle* manuscripts have Cnut succeeding to Mercia, while another, from a northern contributor, simply has 'the north part'.[57]

Contrary to the popular image of a kingdom united under the heirs of Alfred, England was now divided between two rulers. This was not unprecedented, however. Alfred had divided territory with his Viking adversary Guthrum after the Battle of Edington in 878, but Alfred had been giving away that which was not his. Edgar 'the Peaceable' and Eadwig were Anglo-Saxon kings, brothers indeed, who had divided England between them just within living memory of the Olney agreement. Edgar had ruled the Mercian and Northumbrian kingdoms from 957 until his brother's death in 959. In 1016, then, Edmund Ironside became King of the West Saxons, the first since the mid tenth century, and Cnut's control of northern territories may have been recognized as tying in with earlier traditions of joint rulership. Any sense that there was once a planned division of the kingdom could have played into Cnut's hands when he became sole ruler, as he could then have drawn upon the precedent of Edgar's subsequent reunification of the English kingdom following his brother's death.

Cnut did not have to wait long. At the end of November 1016, Edmund, then King of the West Saxons, died after reigning over his territory for just a few weeks. Although he had means, motive and perhaps opportunity, no accusations are made in contemporary sources that Cnut was responsible for Edmund's death. It would be surprising if no one at the time thought it, as some did a century later, though without any clear evidence we should admit it is more likely that Edmund died a natural death, perhaps brought on by the stresses of the year that had passed. It is perhaps telling of the contemporary perception of that year that the *Anglo-Saxon Chronicle* chooses to end the 1016 annal with the death of a king. The Chronicler begins the next year, 1017, with a new king. Cnut was evidently in the right place at the right time. He may well have been in London with the army, as John of Worcester implies (noting that Edmund died in London), though for everything to have worked in his favour Cnut did not need to be.[58] John does suggest that shenanigans were afoot, indicating that Cnut had been misinformed that Edmund accepted him as his successor. But legitimacy was something that could be – and was – gained through the threat of force, particularly when there was no opposition. At least two of Æthelred's surviving sons managed to escape to Flanders that winter, where they seem to have been in Ghent, while the very young sons of Edmund Ironside were sent away, perhaps to the Swedish king with an order to have them killed.[59] They would survive, but only as part of the Hungarian court, where they posed no great threat to Cnut. He had made his bid for power across the kingdom and it had paid off. Cnut was now King of the English.

2
King of the English

There is a paradox to the early years of Cnut's reign in England. On the one hand there seems to have been a surprisingly smooth transition of power to the new kingdom, while on the other, these years were punctuated by bloodletting and violence, at least in some quarters. Some of those living through the time may have looked away from the violence, focusing on the advantages inherent in Cnut's accession, perhaps relieved by the relative stability following the end of a long war. Others were likely to have been acutely aware of the injustices that a takeover of a polity of the size of England entailed. Cnut's first act, the *Anglo-Saxon Chronicle* records, was to divide the kingdom into four, and this act is typical of how Cnut's conquest managed to project a sense of both continuity and change. As the *Chronicle* has it, Wessex was reserved 'for himself', with East Anglia going to Thorkell, Mercia to the man who already held it, Eadric Streona (at least for the moment), and Northumbria to Erik of Lade, a Norwegian in Cnut's service.[1] It appeared to be a reshaping of the mechanisms of power in the Scandinavian mould. During the 1020s Cnut relied on jarls both in Denmark and in Norway,[2] and it looked as though his intention was to govern England along similar lines, with the control of the English kingdom going into the hands of semi-independent earls, equivalent to the Scandinavian jarls. However, as we shall see, Eadric was dead within a year of Cnut's accession and the king's direct rule of Wessex was quickly devolved. Thus the extent to which the division was intended as anything more than a temporary measure is debatable, particularly as the areas controlled by the earls' predecessors, ealdormen, had already been increasing during Æthelred's reign.[3]

Some of the developments were violent, all the same. While later Anglo-Norman historians are more partial in their accounts of the period, sparing no details of Viking atrocities, the *Anglo-Saxon Chronicle* is more dispassionate, neither attributing blame to the new regime nor taking the moral high ground. This relatively sober perspective may have been because the *Chronicle* was written for an audience that included both Viking followers of Cnut and members of the pre-1016 English nobility.[4] Hence while the deaths of important figures must be recorded, it would not have been appropriate for the writer to revel in them. The most significant record in this respect is of the execution in 1017 of four noblemen and the exile, followed by the death, probably in the same year, of Eadwig, son of Æthelred (the *Chronicle* says nothing about what happened to Æthelred's other children or those of Edmund Ironside). This violence had political ends. The death of the notorious Eadric Streona was the first to be mentioned by the *Chronicle*. An Anglo-Norman narrative places Eadric's head on a spike on Tower Hill outside London, suggesting that the execution was later seen as a traitor's death.[5] However, the more contemporary evidence is perhaps significant enough in that Eadric, a chief adviser at Æthelred's court, was often cited as the reason for military defeats during the reigns of both Æthelred and Edmund, and had shared in the very brief four-way division of the kingdom at the start of 1017. Either Eadric had done something that caused Cnut to change his mind and dramatically terminate this agreement or, because he was seen as untrustworthy, he was the victim of a ruthless gameplan that the new king had in mind all along.

The identities of the three other noblemen who were executed indicate that a shift in policy had occurred. One, named Northman, was the son of a western Mercian ealdorman, Leofwine, a man who would later go on to hold office until around 1023 and whose family remained important for much of the century.[6] Another, Æthelweard, was the son of the ealdorman of the western provinces of Somerset, Devon, Cornwall and Dorset. Of Beorhtric, apart from the fact that he was the son of a certain Ælfheah 'of Devonshire', we know little else for certain, though he seems to have been linked to Æthelweard's family.[7]

What we know of where these men came from suggests Cnut's consolidation in the western provinces of the English kingdom, both along the Welsh borders and in the South-West, linked with the rise of a possible kinsman of Æthelmær, Odda of Deerhurst, who may have overseen the treaty made in 1016. Though we should not rule out the possibility that Cnut was flailing out angrily at the wrong people while vainly trying to assert control over powerful families, it is worth thinking about what these acts could have been intended to achieve if they were more than knee-jerk responses to perceived threats. Violent action may have allowed the control of one element within a powerful family while stamping out the potential for opposition by another. In the case of Æthelweard we see another by that name come to the ealdormanry, probably Æthelmær's son-in-law.[8] The violence was more than simply capricious. The young king was emerging as a ruthless figure and probably wished to be seen as such too.

Neither Cnut's mutilation of hostages in 1014 nor his actions in the bloody year of 1017 were unusual in eleventh-century Europe, though. Indeed, they had been a characteristic of Æthelred's reign, even if often blamed on Eadric Streona. In other ways, Cnut did not act as he might be expected to. Other English kings of the era – Eadred (in 948), Eadwig (952), Edgar (969), Æthelred (entering his majority in 986) and, later, Harthacnut (1041) – visited large-scale violence upon cities or whole regions as part of the process of putting down rebellion or disobedience, often early on in their reigns.[9] While Cnut fitted a pattern of English kingship in being comparatively young around the start of his reign in 1017–19, unlike his predecessors he is not recorded as having ravaged a disobedient part of the kingdom.

Perhaps the sheer slog of the campaigns of 1016 had served to quell any appetite Cnut might otherwise have had to make a violent mark upon some unfortunate region of the kingdom, though security was not necessarily guaranteed in these early years. He maintained a large Scandinavian force until 1018 and kept a substantial part of it thereafter. Unrest may have come to the boil later when, as we shall see, Cnut was in Denmark in 1019 but, for the moment, he had pacified his new kingdom.

It would be surprising if there were no hostility to his rule as a result of new Scandinavian settlement. As with the Norman Conquest, and indeed any regime change, a complete shake-up of the court might be expected, and this is reflected in Cnut's executions of members of the English nobility.[10] Wider settlement by newcomers would have had an impact as well; as with the ninth-century migrations to Britain, settlement wasn't just about numbers but a cultural shift took place too, which we will see more of in Chapter 5.[11] Charters are a useful indication of change and its effect at court, and Scandinavian names often appear in royal documents. Recent work on the pre-Conquest English nobility, using the evidence of settlement recorded two generations or so later in Domesday Book, has shown many 'Danish' names in areas of royal influence in the Wessex heartlands of the English kingdom.[12] Some of the names may have been those of housecarls, a group of warriors who provided Cnut with a personal retinue. Although there is evidence that Cnut's predecessors often had warrior retinues too, sometimes including Scandinavian mercenaries, the presence in the king's household of men whose outlook was across the North Sea, with links to and a culture based on the Scandinavian world, was a reminder that Cnut's power was founded on the military muscle provided by such individuals.

There is sparse evidence to show how Cnut projected himself and was perceived by others when he first came to the English throne. There are no royal diplomas that can be reliably dated to the first year of his reign, but there are indications of a coronation ceremony. A legal text dating from 1018 appears to confirm promises made by Cnut, perhaps indicating that, like Henry I and Stephen a century later, he had made oaths at an earlier coronation ceremony.[13] Given the likelihood that Archbishop Wulfstan had drafted the 1018 text, he was probably also responsible for the representation of Cnut's royal authority expressed in an order of coronation service (*ordo*) in 1017.

Where the ceremony took place is not recorded but there are some clues that attest to its importance. It is perhaps revealing that there is no reference to the place frequently used for tenth-century coronations, Kingston-upon-Thames (Surrey), up until Æthelred's coronation of 979.[14] Confusion also remains about whether, a decade after Cnut's death, Edward the Confessor was crowned in Winchester or Canterbury, suggesting that the traditions of royal coronations could be manipulated if the need arose. The circumstances surrounding Cnut's own ascent to power may have presented just such an occasion, which may explain why London could have been chosen. The city had not previously been used for a royal coronation, at least not during the Viking Age, but a record from the late twelfth-century Dean of St Paul's, Ralph de Diceto, indicates that the coronation did take place at his church in London in 1017, presided over by Archbishop Lyfing of Canterbury.[15] Though it does not record the place of coronation (it rarely did), the language of the *Anglo-Saxon Chronicle* resonates with as much gravitas as might be expected for the occasion, with an emphasis on continuity. Using a formula common to the accession of many Anglo-Saxon rulers since the ninth century, the *Chronicle* tells us that Cnut succeeded to 'all the kingdom of the English'.[16]

Another piece of evidence reminds us that we shouldn't think of coronation as something concerning Cnut alone as a ruler. An early eleventh-century manuscript that records the *ordo* of a coronation and makes much of the importance of the role of the queen has been tentatively suggested as dating from the summer of 1017. The details of the role of a queen at a coronation may be our key for seeing the import-ance of the other woman in Cnut's life, Emma of Normandy, the widow of King Æthelred. In her marriage to Cnut she was the only eleventh-century crowned queen married to an English king in the year of his coronation, suggesting that the surviving document, which records a queen's role in the ceremony, related to Cnut and Emma. While details of the *ordo* no longer survive, we can reasonably assume that the occasion of Cnut's coronation may have also served as the wedding of the new king and former queen.[17] If so, and if the event did indeed take place at St Paul's, there may have been some irony in the post-mortem presence at the event of Emma's first husband, Æthelred, who had died in London and was buried in the church. Was Cnut trying to make a point here? It is perhaps significant that, while he made much of the spiritual kindred of deceased members of his new family, Æthelred was not among them and Cnut had little further to do with London.[18]

The first charters that survive from Cnut's reign, from 1018 and 1019, perhaps do so because they were the very first, imbued with the authority of a recently anointed king.[19] These charters are couched in the same confident language of declarative governance that had been used in the time of his predecessor Æthelred. They are signed with phrases such as 'governor of the orb of the English' or 'monarch of all Britain', and Cnut even referred to himself by the Byzantine imperial term *Basileus*. These words echoed the language of tenth-century English kingship and were indicative of Cnut's ambition as a new ruler.[20] Along with such ambition we see the importance of the presence at court – or at least in correspondence with the court – of Archbishop Wulfstan, a figure who had kept the English kingdom on an even keel during the dark days of the later reign of Æthelred.

Wulfstan might be thought the last person to accept a Viking king whose rule was imposed by conquest over an anointed king. The archbishop had railed against Vikings in his 1014 'Sermon of the Wolf' and much of the thrust of his pronouncements in the preceding decade had been concerned with showing how Viking aggression was God's punishment of the English people. Wulfstan was also Bishop of Worcester, in whose see at least one man had lost both his hands 'while a hostage of Danes' – perhaps, as we saw in Chapter 1, as a result of Cnut's actions.[21] Such personal connections might mean that the memory of conquest was painfully alive for a churchman connected to the west Midland nobility.[22] Still, Wulfstan was evidently versed in early medieval realpolitik. His position as archbishop in an area settled by people who still saw themselves as 'Danes' and had close connections across the North Sea, owed much to political pragmatism. Equally, from Cnut's perspective we should remember that he had been driven from the kingdom thanks to the recall of Æthelred from exile in

1014 during an assembly over which Wulfstan presided – an assembly at which Cnut had expected his father to be crowned. Cnut would have had to draw deeply upon his own pragmatism in his dealings with Wulfstan.

Cnut recognized that by retaining Wulfstan he could make a smooth transition, giving him good reason to value his relationship with the archbishop as well as Wulfstan's writings, in which Danish actions appeared divinely ordained.[23] Through Wulfstan, Cnut issued four legal texts during the first five years of his reign. Though there is debate as to whether one could classify them as law codes, all such texts issued under Cnut provide a striking sense of legal declaration, establishing his reputation as a law-making king for centuries to come.[24]

Issuing laws was a demonstration of kingship but it wasn't necessarily ruling, however. With Wulfstan clearly wielding the pen that inscribed the laws, Cnut might unsympathetically be seen as a nodding figurehead uninterested in details as long as the royal coffers remained full. Indeed, that is how some historians have chosen to regard him. But that would be to overlook the effort that had been made to secure the English kingdom in the first place. The smooth manner with which Cnut took control of government indicates careful planning and policy-making. In the first years of his English reign, with his brother Harald either as sole ruler in Denmark or perhaps with Cnut as junior partner in nominally 'shared' rulership,[25] Cnut's main role lay in ruling England. This involved a shift from the traditional means by which Scandinavian rulers had asserted their control on territory in Britain and indeed

Ireland.[26] Cnut did not follow in the footsteps of other Viking rulers, such as, in Northumbria, his namesake Cnut of York (early tenth century), Olaf Sihtricsson (r. 941–4 and 949–52) or Erik 'Bloodaxe' (r. 948–9 and 952–4), nor did he seek to emulate Alfred the Great's rival Guthrum, who established himself in East Anglia at the end of the ninth century. Swein Forkbeard had thought in northern terms, and Cnut's base in Lincolnshire following his father's death, and even his temptation to head north in early 1016, suggest that his original intentions had been to look north to power. But it was a move down south that had settled the matter for Cnut as ruler of England, where he adopted English forms of rulership and in so doing demonstrated that he was far more than merely his father's heir.

In these early years, Cnut needed legitimation. His wife Ælfgifu of Northampton, introduced in Chapter 1, was to remain married to him throughout his reign and that marriage would remain important in Scandinavia, but a union with Queen Emma, widow of Cnut's predecessor Æthelred, gave him the recognition he needed in *English* terms. This was not the savagely symbolic seizure of a conquered king's consort in a moment of triumph, as it might have been had Cnut married Edmund Ironside's widow (who, in any case, was related to the same Mercian family as that of Ælfgifu of Northampton, and whose children were too young to be a threat in 1017). Emma hailed from a dynasty established by a Viking warlord in France a century earlier and which still retained Scandinavian links; she was the sister of Richard II, Duke of Normandy (996–1026), but her position as an English queen may have mattered more. Following the narrative set out in the often misleading *Encomium*, it is sometimes assumed that Emma had left England for Normandy in 1016, but there is more to consider. An imperious demand that Emma be 'fetched', as the *Anglo-Saxon Chronicle* has it, would have been unlikely to have been received favourably if directed towards Normandy.[27] What is more, while Emma may have gone into exile with other members of Æthelred's family in 1013, she had travelled separately and had evidently returned to England by the troubled year of 1016 as she was present during the siege of London.[28] Unlike the æthelings Edward and Alfred, Emma had no opportunity to take refuge on the continent. Emma's encomiast paints a picture of Cnut searching far and wide for a suitable bride before finally finding and wooing Emma in Normandy, but that author was trying to play down the significance of Emma's earlier marriage to Æthelred. If he had shown Emma in England before Cnut's marriage to her in 1017, he would then have had to explain why she was there, and that would have meant admitting to the existence (and status) of the children already born to Æthelred and Emma.

The notion of her being 'fetched' probably belies Emma's interests in her marriage to Cnut. Reference by the Chronicler to Emma being fetched may indicate that there was no need to negotiate with her own family in Normandy. By the time of her marriage to Cnut in the summer of 1017, she had been a widow for more than a year, the period during which remarriage was proscribed by law. Although Emma's own future as a widow and the mother of children whose existence threatened the new king probably left her little room for manoeuvre, there could be no question of coercion;

reinforcing earlier custom, Cnut's own laws upheld the right of women to refuse marriage if they wished.[29]

We have seen how historians have attempted to explain away Cnut's first marriage, to 'the other Ælfgifu', as being 'in the Danish fashion' and thus less meaningful than the marriage contracted to Emma. Those around Emma, and perhaps Emma and Cnut themselves, may have explained the situation in this way to an English audience, had they needed to. Emma had been brought up in Normandy, where dukes of Normandy often had relationships with women from families of Scandinavian settlers while being married to Frankish princesses, so rationalizing the presence of Cnut's first wife in those terms would not have seemed abnormal to Emma.[30] The Encomiast depicts Emma refusing marriage unless Cnut swore an oath that children by her marriage would be accepted as successors, but that is more likely to relate to how, much later in life, Emma wished the situation to have been. In 1017, there was probably no need for negotiation and oath-swearing. Ælfgifu is most likely to have married Cnut in 1013, and she would probably have left England at the time of his own departure in 1014. Only the word of witnesses could determine the validity of that first marriage. Few, including Emma, might wish to draw attention to her existence when Emma was betrothed to Cnut, even if Ælfgifu had returned to England in 1016.[31] We will see more of Cnut's relationship with his first wife in later chapters, but it is perhaps revealing of Cnut's bigamy that the inconvenient truth of the first marriage appears in English sources only after his death, when the English succession was again disputed.

Cnut had much to gain from his marriage to Emma. She controlled properties that had been gifted to her when she married Æthelred, and as the king's widow she would probably have come into possession of many of the familial lands that had been in her husband's hands and might expect to continue to hold them until such time as her children, Æthelred's sons, inherited them.[32] That moment doesn't seem to have come in 1016, and Emma's continuing presence in London suggests that her position as a crowned queen had been accepted by Edmund, Æthelred's son by his first wife. Thus it makes sense that Cnut would also have had to acknowledge the importance of marrying Emma.

Crucially, marriage could also mean a new child for a royal family. Cnut lacked an English heir recognized as an ætheling. While he probably had at least one child, Swein, with Ælfgifu of Northampton by about 1016, and their son Harald 'Harefoot' may even have been born by then too, it is unlikely that either would have been acknowledged in parts of England as being of royal blood so soon after Cnut's accession.[33] A Viking conqueror who had proved himself in war was one thing, but if Cnut had died early in his reign, the English nobility – many of whom had overlooked his succession to Swein in 1014 – would have been unlikely to countenance the succession of an infant son born to Ælfgifu and Cnut who had no other links to the English royal family. After all, Edward and Alfred, the sons of Æthelred and Cnut's new queen, Emma, were still at large, and growing into adulthood just across the Channel. As a legitimate queen representing the continuity of the kingdom, Emma could provide Cnut with an heir of the royal kin.

Producing and keeping new heirs wasn't straightforward, of course. Alfred is the only Anglo-Saxon ruler for whom the emotional impact of the death of a child at an early age is hinted at in a contemporary source,[34] though princely mortality must have been an issue within living memory of Cnut's generation. Edgar had lost his own 'legitimate son' in 971, a matter which had led to a disputed succession during the childhood of Cnut's predecessor, Æthelred. Indeed, the creation of heirs had evidently been a matter of concern for Æthelred, whose first wife's rapid production of a large number of children has led one commentator to wonder whether Æthelred had in fact married twice before Emma.[35] What can be established about Cnut's situation is more difficult to determine, but the presence of Harthacnut with his family in Canterbury in 1023, recorded by the *Anglo-Saxon Chronicle*, indicates that he must have been old enough to travel safely with the court by then. It is reasonable to suppose, therefore, that Emma was pregnant with Harthacnut very soon after her marriage to Cnut in 1017. The birth in 1018 of a son whose mother was the consecrated queen would have given Cnut greater confidence in England's security. From that he could have the scope of ambition to make good his claim to Denmark.[36]

3

From England to Denmark

While England was where Cnut had established his power as a king and demonstrated that he could be regarded as its legitimate ruler, by the time he assembled his witan, probably at Winchester, in Easter 1019, he was now thinking seriously about his future beyond English shores. This matter had probably occupied him for the last year. In 1018 Cnut had held a witan at Oxford that declared a peace between Danes and English. Oxford may have been significant as a place of reconciliation as it is where contemporary evidence survives for a notorious massacre of Danes, perhaps ordered by Æthelred, in 1002.[1] Cnut's notion of peace and reconciliation was determined by another factor, as he first called up what seems to have been the largest payment (*geld*) recorded in the Viking Age. The *Chronicle* records this as £82,500 (£10,500 of which was raised from London alone). A vast sum of money for the time, this was a reminder of what 'peace' could mean in the early eleventh century. The Chronicler's figures seem to have been no mere hyperbole. Though historians have spilled much ink debating whether the figures 'look true' or were the product of imagination,[2] the last two decades of coin finds have tended to indicate that the

Anglo-Saxon kingdom *was* capable of producing such a sizable sum.[3] Although Cnut used a portion of the money to pay off 'some' of his forces, who promptly went to Denmark in 1018, he retained control of a substantial amount.[4] This paid for the services of forty ships and their crews.

What were Cnut's intentions for his remaining fleet? He doesn't seem to have been contemplating wresting power from his brother Harald at that time. Relations between the two seem to have been genuinely fraternal.[5] Although joint rule in Denmark wasn't really on the cards after Swein's death in 1014 – probably because it had been thought, while Swein was alive, that Cnut would have succeeded him in England – both brothers seem to have co-operated. Once Harald was king, he seems to have recognized Cnut as his heir, and the pair had recalled their mother from her exile in 'Sclavonia' (presumably her Polish homeland), where she had been expelled some years earlier for reasons that are now unclear.[6]

So, while Cnut may not have meant his brother ill in 1018, paying off a number of crews had presumably made many a ship's captain a rich man, and the departure for Denmark of these newly enriched leaders may have created instability when they sought influence there. If this was Cnut's plan, it was a gamble as the instability created by dismissing ships' crews made his path to power in Denmark in 1019 rougher than it might otherwise have been. A mid-eleventh-century source refers to unrest following Harald's death, so perhaps Cnut needed at least a display of force to ensure that his succession was accepted.[7] Whatever Cnut's wishes, however, keeping a large fleet in England was expensive and he may have had little choice but to pay off some ships, and it is not impossible that Harald's death at this time was simply a coincidence. Still, as with the seizure of the English kingdom at the end of 1016, Cnut ensured that he was placed to take advantage of the situation. It was a remarkable achievement. Less than three years had passed since he had been accepted as the English king, and a second kingdom now came under his control.

The links between Cnut's Danish kingdom and his English one were strong. North Sea trade had been an important aspect of tenth- and eleventh-century economies but after 1019 it received a further boost that may be seen in the growth of towns in Denmark during Cnut's reign.[8] How much this can be attributed to Cnut is open to question but for many on both sides of the North Sea, the king must have appeared as an embodiment of strength and stability – a figure whose presence allowed trade to flourish and who also directed violence away from a North Sea axis that ran from Scandinavia to England. As we will see, the violence was hardly quelled completely and the Norwegian Sea and the Baltic became areas where Danish royal power and the last vestiges of 'traditional' Viking violence were directed, but Cnut's achievement must have appeared remarkable when he came to the Danish throne in 1019. He had harnessed the aggression of Danish aristocrats and deflected it away from his English realm, strengthening his control of the Danish kingdom in the process. Just as, in England, Cnut looked to the imperial achievements of Æthelred's father, Edgar, in Denmark he was looking to the achievements of his own grandfather, Harald Bluetooth.

Some light may be shone on the policy of Cnut the North Sea ruler by a letter written around 1019, the first that survives from an English monarch to his subjects and which may have been intended to be read out to free men within the localities. While it is not impossible that the letter was written on Cnut's return from Denmark, or even in England by someone writing on the king's behalf, Thorkell – a figure later outlawed by Cnut – seems to be the primary addressee of the letter, alongside Cnut's bishops and archbishops: 'And Earl Thorkell · And all his [i.e. Cnut's] earls'. This would suggest, along with the fact that Thorkell was charged with maintaining justice, that Thorkell was regent in the king's absence. Cnut would otherwise have instructed all his earls directly.[9] Moreover, the record in the *Anglo-Saxon Chronicle* of the king's departure for Denmark in 1019 is important, and we may see the letter as the evidence of the strength of the king's authority; a king who was absent from the kingdom could none the less still rule, because the systems of law and government, which operated in his name, still functioned effectively.[10]

Aside from following in his predecessors' footsteps in declaring in the letter that he was acting in zealous pursuit of God's law, Cnut stated how he was protecting his subjects from external threats with his ('my') money. The audacity of this claim is remarkable given that the dangers to the kingdom had once come from armies led by Cnut and by Thorkell. Many ships' crews had probably found themselves underemployed after 1016 – a dangerous state of affairs that Cnut's *geld* of 1018 may have been intended to address. Evidently other actions had been required, however, particularly if some felt they hadn't received their fair share. Thietmar of Merseburg's grateful acknowledgement that Cnut destroyed a pirate fleet of thirty ships, presumably somewhere in the North Sea in 1018, shows that the king had a broad strategic vision, with the protection of trade routes being in both English and Danish interests.[11] In his letter, Cnut evidently needed to justify his (expensive) actions to his audience, suggesting that the balance of power was linked to consent in England, as laid out in a legal agreement made in Oxford in 1018.[12] The letter shows the continuity of earlier relationships that built on the kingship of Cnut's predecessors, Æthelred and his father Edgar. This should not be read as some dewy-eyed Whig interpretation of power held through consent, but seen in terms of the parameters within which eleventh-century kings had to act and an acceptance by magnates that a ruler had to be seen as *primus inter pares* if he were to govern effectively. Thus, despite the money that Cnut was evidently extracting from the kingdom, he was still extracting it as *his* money by right. We can see in the letter, too, the notion that the protection of the English was something ultimately achievable. Allusions to past and future also reminded Cnut's audience that protecting the people was something that he could do while Æthelred, and indeed Edmund Ironside, had not.

The creation of a sense of continuity in an apparently stable relationship may have stemmed from the influence of Archbishop Wulfstan, who seems to have had a hand in the composition of the letter. Notably the letter survives in a York Gospel book and presents the king as a good Christian ruler, emphasizing his legitimacy as an English king for whom the deliverance of the kingdom had come through God's will – despite the irony that many of those who had brought the kingdom to its knees had been Cnut's men. It is also ironic that a letter sent from outside the English kingdom, written while Cnut was engaged in taking the Danish throne, should have resulted in such a clear statement of *English* rulership. Though the implicit threat to the English people, that they behave, rings out beneath the wording of the text, without this letter we would have had far less sense of Cnut as an English ruler. He might otherwise be filed simply under the category of 'foreign conqueror'. Interestingly, neither the *Chronicle* nor the letter make clear mention of Cnut assuming the throne of the Danish kingdom. To an English audience what presumably mattered were declarations of English legitimacy. It was probably not insignificant that since the days of Æthelwulf, the father of Alfred, Cnut was the first ruler to go overseas and *remain* ruler and, given that Æthelwulf lost part of his kingdom to a rebellious son upon his return, Cnut was clearly powerful and confident in ways that were new to his English subjects and the North Sea world to which they belonged.

Having secured the Danish throne in 1019, Cnut had returned to his English kingdom by Easter 1020. Scarcely a year had passed since he had last been in England. His first action now was to respond to unrest that appeared to have flared up in the West Country. At an assembly at Cirencester, Gloucestershire, he ordered the outlawry of a certain Eadwig, nicknamed (perhaps because he shared the name of, or even claimed to be, a son of Æthelred) 'King of the Ceorls' (i.e. king of the peasants), and the West Country ealdorman

Æthelweard.[13] The threat of royal justice to which Cnut referred in his letter to the English people could now be seen to have been carried out. We don't know if he had to hurry back from Denmark because he received the news of unrest or whether he simply brought the business into the agenda of an assembly that was already scheduled to happen.

There was clearly a need to demonstrate Cnut's domination of the English kingdom. Later that year, perhaps even on the 18 October anniversary of the battle itself, Cnut returned, with Thorkell, to the Essex battlefield of Assandun, where a minster church was founded. Ostensibly such a church was to enable people to pray for the souls of those who had died in the battle and it is likely that, as the *Anglo-Saxon Chronicle* refers to the presence of Wulfstan, the archbishop's sermon on the dedication of a church was written for the occasion.[14] In confirmation of its royal status, Cnut appointed his own chaplain to the church. Prayer for the souls of both sides who had died in battle might be meaningful, but when expressed by the victor, like Franco's 'Valley of the Fallen', a monument to 'both sides' who had died in Spain's Civil War of 1936–9, or indeed King William's abbey at Battle (Sussex), such sentiments tend to have a triumphal ring. Assandun would later cease to mean much as a minster church and indeed because of this there is some uncertainty about its precise location. While this may have been because there was no monastic community to provide continuity, the minster's decline suggests that it remained intimately linked with Cnut's message of domination and thereafter lost its point.

That message of domination may also have been projected

by the record that the king and his foremost earl, both major players in the conquest of 1016, were together for the dedication at Assandun – a former moment of glory relived. By 1021, their relationship had seriously deteriorated. According to the *Anglo-Saxon Chronicle*, Thorkell was 'outlawed'.[15] It is not certain whether this was from England or Denmark, and indeed we do not even know why Thorkell was outlawed – perhaps he had failed to act against the opposition that had surfaced while he was regent – though the *Chronicle* is more likely to have been recording an outlawry from England.

As the son of a 'petty king' of Skåne (Scania) and hence a royal claimant to a key territory only recently incorporated into the Danish kingdom, Thorkell would have presented a powerful rival to Cnut. As political players in the region, both men had a stake in the interests of different groups contesting control in the Baltic. Cnut had close links with his maternal family. His sister, probably the 'Santslaue' recorded in a Winchester *Liber Vitae* as 'sister of Cnut, our king', was married to a king of the Wends, while his mother was a sister of Bolesław Chobry, the Polish ruler and a rival to a group of warriors based at a fortress at Wolin on the River Oder.[16] Thorkell seems to have been linked with this group, identified in later legends and remembered for their close bonds as the Jomsvikings. Perhaps he and Cnut became more closely involved in Baltic affairs as their relationship soured.

The *Anglo-Saxon Chronicle* provides a clue. Cnut's departure for 'Wihtland', recorded in the 'D' version of the *Chronicle*'s entry for 1022, is sometimes read as a voyage across the Solent to the Isle of Wight, but uncertainties of interpretation like this plague the surviving documents. Seen in the context of the politics of the developing Danish kingdom, it is perhaps more appropriate to read Wihtland as a reference to the land of the Wends rather than as the Isle of Wight, particularly as another version of the *Chronicle* notes that, in the following year, 'King Cnut came back to England', an event which would hardly need recording if he had just journeyed across the Solent.[17]

During Thorkell's absence from England, Cnut seems to have renegotiated his relationship with other English nobles. Among these, a previously little-known nobleman from Sussex, Godwine, was awarded the title of earl before Cnut left for Denmark in 1019. He is described in a mid-eleventh-century source as 'earl [*dux*] and office-bearer [*baiulus*] of almost all the kingdom', suggesting that he had been promoted to a position that would allow him to play the role of kingmaker a generation later in the aftermath of Cnut's death. Godwine's star was rising at Cnut's court even as early as 1019–20, when he may have proved himself with service overseas; he certainly benefited from involvement in a campaign in 1022–3.[18] Godwine may have had value of his own if he had inherited ships from his father, Wulfnoth – who seems to have commanded ships from a newly built English fleet in 1009, during the reign of Æthelred. This had been a disastrous moment for Æthelred's kingdom, but if these ships were later commanded by Godwine, some of them could well have been seaworthy enough to be of use to Cnut a decade later.

The *Anglo-Saxon Chronicle* records that Cnut and Thorkell were reconciled in Denmark before Cnut's return to

England in 1023, when he was away on campaign, but the timing of the translation of the relics of Archbishop Ælfheah of Canterbury may reveal something of the waning of Thorkell's star in England. Ælfheah had been martyred at the hands of Thorkell's army in 1012 and his mortal remains had been at St Paul's in London since then, but it was in 1023 that the decision was taken (the saint made his wishes known, we are told) for the relics to return home to Canterbury.[19] First, however, the 'D' version of the *Chronicle*, telling of events in Denmark prior to Cnut's return to England the same year, relates that he and Thorkell were reconciled, with each man being entrusted with the care of the other's son (perhaps as a symbolic guarantee of the deal that had been brokered), and Denmark (or part of it) was entrusted to Thorkell. Only then, back in England, were the saint's relics translated.

This might have made the translation a reconciliation of Church, king and an important Danish magnate, but there is a hitch in reading events in that manner as Thorkell, now 'entrusted' with Denmark, does not seem to have returned to England. Though other Scandinavians were still in high positions at court and Cnut had to acknowledge Thorkell's Danish importance, he was evidently unwelcome in England, where Godwine, who had strong Canterbury connections, had risen to the top. Although there are obvious stereotypes in the account of the translation, it links Thorkell to the martyrdom of the archbishop in 1012.[20] The account of the martyrdom appears to include a representation of Thorkell's enmity towards Cnut, and the act of translating the saint may also have been undertaken at a point when Thorkell's influence in England was low in order to contrast Cnut's

Christianity with the apparently pagan actions of Thorkell's army (no matter that Thorkell himself is unlikely to have been personally responsible for Ælfheah's death).

While the account of Saint Ælfheah's translation casts doubt upon the genuineness of the reconciliation in English terms, Thorkell doesn't seem to have held on to the regency of Denmark for long after 1023 as he disappears from the historical record soon after that.[21] A fragmented picture might be pieced together through a complicated web of marriage negotiations from around that time: Cnut married his sister Estrith to a Danish nobleman, Ulf Thorgilsson, around 1022, when Ulf was in England, and Ulf's sister was married to Godwine, perhaps around the same time.[22] Thus, while Godwine became Cnut's man in England, Ulf was Cnut's Danish regent by 1026. Where was Thorkell in all this? The sources are limited enough to posit that he hadn't been appointed regent of *all* of Denmark, and the *Chronicle* was simply rendering his return to Skåne in terms that made sense to an English audience. However, the reason for the Danish regency becoming available does not have to be attributed to this or to Cnut ordering Thorkell's death. While Cnut's record for disposing of potentially troublesome opponents was already enviable by the mid 1020s, this may be an occasion on which to give him the benefit of the doubt. It is possible that Thorkell simply died soon after 1023 from some illness, a fact which would explain his disappearance from the sources, as well as the survival of the son whom Cnut had entrusted to Thorkell (this was probably Swein; Harthacnut was in England at the time of the translation of Saint Ælfheah, and his half-brother, Harald

Harefoot, may have been too young in 1023). Whatever had happened to Thorkell, no matter what was made of their apparent reconciliation, Cnut is unlikely to have shed many tears for a man who had been his rival for so long.

Cnut's relationship with Thorkell may have affected how he dealt with Ulf, whose career as regent of Denmark was cut short. Cnut had him killed for treason, probably in or just after 1026.[23] The experiences of a decade in power may have given him a suspicious mind but, as Ulf and his brother Eilaf allied themselves with what the *Anglo-Saxon Chronicle* refers to as 'a very great army' from Sweden in 1026, Cnut would have been right to be wary.[24] This army, along with that of King Olaf Haraldsson of Norway, fought Cnut's forces at 'Holy River', a place either in Skåne (then in Denmark) or Uppland, in the heart of Swedish territory, both of which, unhelpfully, had a river by the name of Helgeå (i.e. 'Holy River').[25] Although Cnut's skalds later hailed his military prowess at the battle, the *Anglo-Saxon Chronicle* records that the Swedes 'held the field'.[26] We will see more of Cnut's relations with Norwegians and Swedes, but he may have needed to seek reconciliation once again with his Danish opponents, if only for a short time. We hear nothing of Eilaf in English sources, after the battle, though a Welsh chronicle – the *Brut y Tywysogion* ('Chronicle of the Princes'), which had an interest in Eilaf because he raided Wales in the early 1020s – records that he fled England after Cnut's death,[27] so he would have had to have returned to England in the aftermath of the battle at Holy River. If Cnut was reconciled with Ulf, it did not last. According to Danish tradition, Ulf was killed in the precincts of Roskilde

Cathedral in Denmark. The spilling of blood on holy ground would be serious enough to warrant a display of contrition, and a gift to Roskilde may have been Cnut's recompense to his sister for her husband's death. Politically and personally, however, he had yet again shown that he could be ruthless when the occasion required, even within his own family.

With maintenance of a realm spread across a wide area relying to such a large extent on the politics of family relations, four known children for Cnut – two with Queen Emma, and two with Ælfgifu of Northampton – seems a remarkably low number by the standards of the age. While tenth-century English rulers often had numerous sisters and broods of daughters to marry off to the crowned heads of Europe, Cnut held together his North Sea realms with just these four offspring. Ælfgifu of Northampton continued to play an important role after his marriage to Emma. We cannot be certain that she was in Denmark for all of the 1010s and 1020s; the inscription of 'Ælfgifu' alongside that of 'Imma Regina' in Thorney Abbey's *Liber Vitae* suggests that she had once visited there with a family group, though the manuscript is not contemporary with the 1020s.[28] As a list of names written around 1100, it certainly should not be used as evidence that Cnut was present at Thorney with both wives at the same time. He presumably needed a royal representative in Denmark after 1019. As Ælfgifu bore him two sons, Swein and Harald Harefoot, these would have constituted a useful political presence in his Scandinavian realm.[29] However, while Harald succeeded his father on the English throne in 1035 and Swein could nominally rule Norway on his father's behalf in 1030, neither boy would have been old enough by 1019, and it would appear that Ælfgifu bore no more living children after, at the latest, the early 1020s. Tales recorded soon after 1035 of Harald's illegitimacy, and even that he was the son of a servant, imply that Cnut was inattentive to his first wife and their children, even by the standards of medieval kingship.[30]

Likewise, Cnut's Scandinavian interests must have limited the opportunities for he and Emma to conceive a child during his time at the English court. The fragmentary sources again make it difficult to establish the course of events, but the fact that there were two legitimate children of Cnut and Emma corresponds with the limits put on the opportunities for conception and full-term pregnancy by the king's North Sea itinerary. He was present in England between 1017 and 1019, a time which evidently saw the birth of Harthacnut, who was old enough to be noted in Canterbury in 1023. If Harthacnut – the 'Hard Knot', named after an earlier Danish king but also evoking Cnut's own 'Knot' name – were conceived soon after Cnut and Emma's marriage and born early enough in 1018, another child could well have been conceived before Cnut's departure for Denmark in 1019 (wet-nursing could increase the birth rate for medieval royals). None the less, a period between Cnut's return in 1020 and his departure for Wihtland in 1022 seems to be more likely for the birth of his and Emma's daughter, Gunnhild, who would then have been about fourteen or fifteen when she married Henry, son of the Holy Roman Emperor in 1036.[31] Cnut was evidently present in England between about 1023 and 1025, which would have given the opportunity for more children to be conceived. Emma, however, was older than Cnut, presumably at least thirty-five by this stage, and any pregnancy resulting from such a liaison would have been what is now considered to be 'late', with added risks of miscarriage. Whether or not Emma conceived another child with Cnut after 1023, none – notwithstanding Victorian traditions of a drowned daughter – is known to have survived. Of course, these observations would be meaningless if Emma had ever accompanied her husband to Scandinavia. However, given her significance in the legitimation of the English realm for Cnut, and Ælfgifu's probable role in Denmark and then Norway, it is likely that the North Sea provided a natural barrier between Cnut and his wives, and that his liaisons with Emma were occasional for much of the 1020s.

Still, the king spent no more time in Denmark after 1028. Rather than relying on a jarl to act as regent, Cnut's son Harthacnut, no more than eight years old, was sent to Denmark around 1026 as a token of direct authority in the paternal kingdom.[32] Though it was not uncommon for early medieval rulers to suffer the experience in childhood of the death or expulsion of their mother from court, Cnut must surely have drawn on memories of his own mother's expulsion by Swein Forkbeard when he ordered his son to Denmark. Evidence of Queen Emma's later communication to her daughter Gunnhild suggests that she had grown up near her mother in England rather than in Denmark[33] but from his arrival in the heat of the crisis of 1026–7, Harthacnut was to become his father's man in Denmark. After 1028, for the rest of Cnut's reign, father and son would not see each other again.

4
Wider Still, and Wider

The years from 1026 to 1030 proved crucial for Cnut as a North Sea ruler. While he had not won the glorious victory at Holy River that he might have hoped, the wider campaign was evidently having some success: at the very least, he had held off the alliance of Swedes, Norwegians and rogue Danes ranged against him. 'The gallant kings,' Cnut's skald Sighvat was able to claim, referring to Olaf Haraldsson and the Swedish ruler Anund Jacob, 'could not entice Denmark to them by warfare.'[1] One later account even suggests that Cnut had played a strategic ace by blockading the sea lane between Skåne and the Danish island of Sjælland, preventing the Norwegians from using their ships to get back to Norway and thus forcing them to trudge home across Sweden in the northern winter.[2] Sadly, no contemporary source provides enough detail to help us judge whether this was indeed what happened or if it was simply saga embellishment, but whatever Cnut had really done to secure his position, a long game was paying off. In 1027, a new Holy Roman Emperor, Conrad, was to be crowned in Rome. Inconvenient though it might be to take time out to go to Rome in the midst of a campaign, if Cnut did not attend the coronation his absence might be seen as a snub to a powerful German neighbour. His enemies' advances at least delayed, Cnut travelled to Rome in 1027. His experience of being seen in a major imperial ceremony evidently changed his sense of what a king could be:[3] the hegemony he held as ruler of two kingdoms had the potential to be transformed into something that was imperial in outlook, if not an empire in itself.

It is reasonable to suppose that Cnut would have been honourably received by his English subjects residing in Rome and by Conrad, whose German territory he had to cross in order to reach the Eternal City. Indeed, the two rulers probably began marriage negotiations for their children. Gunnhild, Cnut and Emma's daughter, was eventually married to Conrad's son Henry in 1036 and a promise of marriage of the young girl, perhaps no more than six years old in 1027, could have provided Cnut with the political recognition he needed.[4] He had seen old Roman cities in England but eleventh-century Rome still had the power to impress. The imperial sense of majesty had evidently affected Cnut when, on the way back from Rome, he sent the second of his surviving letters to his English subjects, who seem to have been under the regency of more than one authority. The letter refers to those 'councillors to whom I have entrusted the councils of the kingdom'.[5] It thus acted as a reminder that Cnut remained king, indicating that, after he had been to Denmark once more, he would return to England, but it also went a step further, bringing the English kingdom into an imperial realm. The Latin text of the letter claims Cnut as *'rex totius Angliae et Denemarcie et Norreganorum et partis Suanorum'*, 'King of All

England and Denmark and of the Norwegians and of part of the Swedes'.[6] For the first time, it looked as though this statement went beyond mere hyperbole.

The aspirations were audacious but they were within Cnut's grasp. Indeed, his claim to authority over 'part of the Swedes' led early generations of modern historians to highlight the pan-Scandinavian nature of his rule.[7] Those historians were right – after a fashion. Cnut did control territory in what is now part of Sweden, in Skåne. However, as we have seen, that region was already considered by the late tenth century to be part of the Danish kingdom rather than Sweden. Beyond Skåne, Cnut's control of the eleventh-century kingdom in eastern Sweden was more ephemeral than the historians gave him credit for. The Encomiast, normally liberal with praise for Cnut, perhaps reflects this as there is no mention of Swedish affairs in the *Encomium*. The Swedes – known at the time as the *Svearr* – over whom kings of Denmark claimed sovereignty prior to Cnut's reign had rejected his brother Harald, presumably after hearing of the death of Swein Forkbeard.[8] As we have seen, the Swedes seem to have been on the offensive against Cnut, perhaps because he had been trying to extend his influence in the Baltic. He had not made good this control by 1027, though he fought battles against Swedes in 1026, including at Holy River, in an attempt to assert control of disputed territory. Given that the Norwegian ruler and Danish renegades were willing to side with King Anund Jacob of Sweden, the battle may not have been fought on Cnut's terms, though one likely site of the battle, Uppland in Sweden, was well outside Danish territory and might suggest that Cnut's forces had at least advanced before they were met in battle.

In any case, could Cnut justifiably claim to rule even 'part' of the Swedes? Many Swedish runestones commemorate Swedish warriors in his or his father's service, and these may be our key.[9] A large number of those warriors referred to as 'thegns' and 'drengs' were from an area that may have been tributary to Danish authority around 1000. Drengs seem to have been younger than thegns and perhaps had not yet settled before they died, so declarations of their warrior status on the runestones may show that they still accepted Cnut's royal lordship after returning to Uppland.[10] In this context, personal lordship helps to explain how and why Cnut could claim kingship over some Swedes at a crucial point in his involvement in Scandinavian affairs, while a few years after his death that expression of overlordship had been forgotten. Perhaps some of Cnut's Swedes served him directly in Swedish territory against Anund Jacob just as Norwegian warriors served Cnut's jarls in Norway. That would hardly be surprising, given the complex webs of alliances and enmities that evolved in eleventh-century Scandinavia and the wealth that Cnut could offer to those following him.

An even more contentious issue for the Danish kingdom was its control of the developing kingdom of Norway, claimed since the mid tenth century by Cnut's grandfather. The Jelling Runestone raised by Harald Bluetooth declares that he won Norway as well as Denmark, so with the control of Norway central to a display of Danish kingship, the loss of whatever power the Danes held in Norway after the death of Swein in 1014 must have been keenly felt. Olaf

Haraldsson, a warlord who had served in London under Æthelred, became Cnut's principal Norwegian opponent. He appears to have gained control of the kingdom at around the same time that Cnut was making good his claim in England.[11] Cnut had been occupied elsewhere for much of the 1010s and 1020s, as we have seen, but the matter of Norway was becoming more pressing. A Norwegian force, probably under Olaf himself, was at Holy River and Olaf had married the daughter of King Anund Jacob of Sweden, suggesting an anti-Cnut alliance that posed a real threat. When Cnut returned from Rome in 1027, taking the initiative against King Olaf must have been uppermost in his mind. His claim to rule the Norwegians, premature though it might have been in 1027, made perfect sense.

Cnut may have returned to England by the end of 1027 as, according to some versions of the *Anglo-Saxon Chronicle*, he took a fleet of fifty ships with him from England to Norway in 1028. There was no battle and, with enough Norwegian jarls willing to side with Cnut (as Erik of Lade had done back in the 1010s), Olaf fled, eventually ending up, temporarily, in Russia. As we have seen, Cnut's sense of imperial prestige may have been invigorated by his visit to Rome in the spring of the previous year, and control of Norway was perhaps a fitting triumph for him, as well as a suitable return for the enormous investment needed to maintain a show of strength. Going from Sweden to Rome, from Rome to England and from England to Norway would have involved land and sea travel of over three thousand miles in the course of just over a year, an average distance of some ten miles a day. This was pan-European travel on a par with that of Charlemagne over two centuries before. Charlemagne, though, had done little to make himself master of the sea. If the massive 'Roskilde 6' ship, which dates from these years, was indeed built for Cnut, its construction from timber from the Oslo Fjord takes on further significance in the light of the king's travels and the symbolic importance accorded by seafarers at the time to where a king's ship was built and by whom.[12] Here was a mighty instrument of Cnut's power by which he could rule North Sea realms, built from timber taken from the heart of a territory that had come back into the hands of a Danish king.

In Norway, Cnut used his wealth to buy the support he needed, and he could put a price on Olaf's head.[13] With Håkon, son of Jarl Erik, as his regent in the conquered territory, Cnut seems to have turned to his father's policy of ruling Norway through a local jarl. It was a policy that could have worked had Håkon not drowned the following year. Later sources add colour to the *Anglo-Saxon Chronicle*'s sparse account of his drowning. John of Worcester relates a plot against Cnut, with the king contriving to have Håkon exiled, along with his wife Gunnhild (the daughter of Cnut's sister, perhaps 'Santslaue', and a Wendish king recorded by John as 'Wyrtgeorn'), noting that Håkon may have been killed in Orkney. This detail may be corroborated by a twelfth-century Norwegian chronicle that suggests Håkon was drowned in the Pentland Firth while he was bringing his bride (who survived) back from England.[14] Was this another example of Cnut's ruthlessness in disposing of a potential rival? Probably not. In the face of the likelihood of Olaf's return, Håkon was too valuable a strand in Cnut's web of alliances, and the only information that we might draw from this, beyond the marriage of Cnut's niece, is that Orkney was part of Norway at this point and that a jarl ruling Norway also had to deal with the jarls of Orkney.

With Håkon dead, Olaf returned with an army to Norway, where he attempted to reclaim his crown. Cnut's silver had done its work, however. Olaf's support was not universal across Norway, particularly in the central belt of the Trøndelag, where the jarls of Lade had held authority. Met by his enemies at Stiklestad in July 1030, Olaf was killed in the ensuing battle. Cnut, however, did not fall back on his policy of appointing a native jarl to Norway. After Håkon's death, he perhaps did not regard any jarl as trustworthy enough to be given the task – his actions over the previous two decades show that he had, after all, perceived a good number of nobles as traitors to him during the last two decades. Moreover, he tended to appoint jarls through marriage to an extended family network and this was now stretched thinly (his daughter Gunnhild may already have been betrothed by then to the son of the Holy Roman Emperor). Perhaps reflecting a change in royal policy, Cnut appointed his son Swein as regent, under the auspices of Swein's mother, Ælfgifu. The harsh rule of 'Ælfgifu's Time' is recalled with bitterness in Norwegian historical writings a century later. Though we should always be sensitive to the exaggeration of folk memory, particularly given that the rule of a foreign-born woman might be regarded unsympathetically by male writers, the evidence for the later repeal of laws that are likely to have been made during this period suggests that the foreign rule was unpopular.[15]

Cnut's empire had reached its practical limits, though there was still work to be done to consolidate it.

On returning to England, Cnut directed his attention towards Scotland for the first time since territory was ceded to the King of the Scots in 1018. The *Anglo-Saxon Chronicle* indicates that in 1031 Cnut went to Scotland 'and the king of the Scots surrendered to him'.[16] This probably took place without a battle, but Cnut, with a large fleet at his disposal, presumably made a strong show of force. One *Chronicle* version indicates that, along with King Malcolm, 'two other [regional] kings, Mælbæth and Iehmarc', also submitted to Cnut.[17] Although there is confusion about the date, as the *Chronicle* relates the submission to Cnut's return from Rome (thus dating it to 1027 or 1028), the other Scottish rulers named by the Chronicler – one of whom, 'Mælbæth', more familiar to us as Shakespeare's 'Macbeth' – were active after 1030, suggesting that the Chronicler's date of 1031 was correct. Cnut's insistence upon a receipt of submission – a formal ceremony – would have been an attempt to prevent his Norwegian opponents from gaining Scottish support at the point when Norway (and thus Shetland, Orkney and Caithness) came within his domains.[18] Cnut had, almost by default, reinstated a British hegemony enjoyed by Anglo-Saxon kings of the early and mid tenth century. But why did Scotland or Britain not feature in Cnut's self-representation when he wrote his letter from Rome in 1027? There is some logic to this. Norway, which was mentioned in the letter, had been claimed by Danish kings, and claim to a lordship over some Swedes made sense in the context of that year. Scottish overlordship only came into focus after Norway was taken by Cnut.

We can see how an idea of empire began to form during the course of the latter part of Cnut's reign by the *Encomium*'s claim, made after his death, that he was 'Emperor of Five Kingdoms': Denmark, England, Wales, Scotland and Norway.[19] As we have seen, Swedish lordship had ceased to be significant after his death, which may explain the absence of Swedes (or part of them) from this list, but the third of the kingdoms named, Wales, gets little mention in Cnut's reign itself. An attack in the early 1020s on Wales by Eilaf, then a Mercia-based earl, may have been carried out with royal approval, though this could equally have been carried out independently of Cnut's authority.[20] In any case, it was hardly enough for the *Encomium*'s claim of overlordship. While Wales was of concern during Cnut's reign, it was almost certainly beyond his control, perhaps because there was no single hegemony over the patchwork of small and medium-sized kingdoms that then constituted Wales.[21] When the *Encomium* was written years later, Wales was an issue of greater concern to the English kingdom, and a more definable hegemony had come into being. The new King of Gwynnedd, Gruffudd ap Llywellyn, began reasserting the power of his kingdom after Cnut's death. The serious defeat he inflicted on the Mercians in 1039 is perhaps what caused the notion of Cnut's Welsh overlordship to be stressed, even exaggerated, when the *Encomium* was written in the early 1040s.

The Viking kingdom of Dublin was outside Cnut's direct control, though he may have made alliances with the people of Dublin. As one commentator has noted, Dublin's traders had vested interests in the financial opportunities that Cnut's North Sea territories gave them, but Irish links with Norway also meant that he could never afford to be complacent.[22] Beyond such observations, however, it is difficult to know Cnut's intentions in the Irish Sea zone, and the picture remains almost wholly mysterious.

Yet one area within the Anglo-Scandinavian world lay firmly outside Cnut's sphere of influence, illustrating his need to keep abreast of developments on different fronts. The duchy of Normandy was a major power in France by the early eleventh century and its dukes hosted Æthelred's sons, the æthelings, the exiled Edward and Alfred, as honoured guests. Such kingship in exile could be politically sensitive. It may explain why, despite Cnut's focus on controlling Scandinavian realms from 1019 to 1030, the political centre of gravity of his kingship ultimately began to shift back to the south of England during the 1030s.[23] A careful balancing act may have meant that Normandy had not been a threat at first. At least one skaldic poet had visited Duke Richard II of Normandy, suggesting that his court retained Scandinavian links and shared many of the same interests as that of Cnut, and there is some evidence that Cnut's marriage to Emma may have allowed the brothers-in-law to have enjoyed reasonably cordial relations (Cnut may even have granted land to the Norman monastery of Fécamp[24]). However, Normandy was drifting away from Cnut after a change of regime in 1027.[25] Robert the Magnificent, Richard's son, came to power following a coup launched against his elder brother. Perhaps sensing changes in Anglo-Norman relations, and finding himself with an unmarried sister in the form of Estrith, whose husband Ulf had died after the Battle of Holy River, Cnut proposed marrying her to the Norman duke.

The picture is, admittedly, confused, as Adam of Bremen's account has it that the duke *actually* married Cnut's sister, then repudiated her, then went on pilgrimage (which he is known to have done, but not until much later, in 1035), while Estrith was then free to marry Ulf (her former husband, who would have already been dead by then!).[26] As Robert is mistaken in this account for his father Richard II, it may be realistic to read this as a marriage negotiation that came to nothing or was turned down.[27] Whatever the case, Robert seems to have been becoming more aggressive towards his immediate neighbours, so an attempt to tie him to Cnut's family through marriage would have been sensible. In Normandy, Edward, the son of Æthelred, remained with his brother at the ducal court, witnessing and even claiming to be the English king when he signed Robert's charters. The duke even appears to have launched an invasion of England around 1033–4 on behalf of his English cousins. According to the eleventh-century Norman chronicler William of Jumièges, the Norman fleet foundered in a storm off the Channel Islands but the threat it posed to Cnut's kingdom must have been serious. A charter of 'King Edward' made at some point during Duke Robert's reign for the Norman monastery of Mont-Saint-Michel provides context, as this is where the invasion fleet was said to have ended up. Edward's offer of land in Cornwall to the monastery may help us to understand that he was grateful for his Norman support.[28] Despite the skalds extolling his Scandinavian kingship, Cnut seems to have remained largely in the south of England after 1031. The threat of the return of Æthelred's sons, now actively supported by a far stronger Norman ducal house, would have ensured that Cnut could never rest assured of a safe succession in England.

Such problems in the south of the realm in the 1030s had implications for the security of Danish rule in Norway. Cnut's first wife Ælfgifu and their son Swein faced opposition centred around a rapidly developing cult of Saint Olaf Haraldsson, whose death at the hands of 'pagan' enemies at Stiklestad in 1030 was portrayed as martyrdom in the politically charged circumstances of direct Danish rule. Buoyed by this, Olaf's son Magnus returned from exile in 1034 and seized power.[29] Ælfgifu and Swein fled Norway: Ælfgifu ended up in England within a year and Swein predeceased his father. It may be no coincidence that Magnus seems to have acted within about a year of the abortive Norman-sponsored invasion. As would happen in the much better known events of 1066 a generation later, with political interests linked from the Channel to the North Sea and beyond, the effects of events in one place could be felt elsewhere. Cnut's imperial kingship relied on the force of personality, one man able to make his presence felt in places hundreds of miles apart through ensuring personal connections of fosterage and marriage. Perhaps the weight of what he had built was beginning to be too much for such structures of power, though before the empire is dismissed as a house of cards, there is one last element of Cnut's rule that needs to be considered.

5

Into Realms Beyond

Is Cnut in Hell? In a profound investigation into the motivations of an early tenth-century usurpation, the historian Geoffrey Koziol asked the same question of the Frankish king Robert I, concluding with the answer: 'I don't know. But I believe the question mattered to him, and that it mattered to him should matter to us.'[1] The fate of his eternal soul mattered to Cnut, too. Like Robert's, his rule came through usurpation and bloody conquest; but unlike Robert, who can be easily read as a pious prince in the mould of his Frankish contemporaries, narratives about Cnut normally make much of the 'old Viking' world of the Danish prince, as if ideas of Christian salvation were something to which a warlord would simply pay lip service before moving on to more interesting matters.

If we think of Cnut in these terms, we do him and those around him a disservice. Indeed, the Bishop of Chartres admitted to this mistake when he wrote to the king, thanking him for a gift while apologizing for having believed him to be pagan.[2] By the standards of his day, there is much to suggest that Cnut was a pious king and, if the number of records of his death in English monasteries is anything to go by, he may even be the most likely of

Anglo-Saxon kings to have gained salvation. That may seem a jarring, even blasphemous statement. What about his bigamy? What about the claims of Alfred the Great, Edgar or the saintly Edwards? Granted, Norman saint-making after 1066 might be important for at least Edward the Confessor, but Cnut was the only pre-Conquest ruler since Æthelwulf to travel to and from Rome while king. If such achievements and the number of monks and clergy praying for Cnut counted for anything in contemporary theology, the words of his 1027 letter indicate that at least someone in his party understood the importance of travelling to Rome – 'to pray for the redemption of my sins and the salvation of my kingdoms and of the peoples who are subject to my rule'[3] – and presumably someone must have informed him of the redemptive power of making such a pilgrimage.[4] In terms of its sheer scale (and there are few other pre-Conquest kings who were publicly concerned with the passage of English pilgrims), Cnut's record could not be beaten. A range of churches were favoured by his patronage, not just in the royal heartlands of Wessex but also from Essex, the old eastern Danelaw of East Anglia, the west Midlands and Durham, as well as Christ Church, Canterbury. York does not seem to have been on this list after Wulfstan's death in 1023, but even here, a sensible policy seems to have prevailed: Cnut does not seem to have interfered with the affairs of the see, suggesting he was aware of the important control it had over churches in the North, where royal authority could be perceived as distant.[5] There were good reasons for the presentation of Cnut as a Christian monarch. Aside from Æthelstan (924–39),

Cnut's role in conquests in England and Norway, and interference in the politics of the Baltic, must have meant that he had more blood on his hands than any other English king of the Viking Age, so the Christian endorsement of his reign mattered. It probably mattered more and more as he grew older.

We see how in one of the most arresting and famous depictions of Cnut, dating from 1031, which turned out to be late in his reign. The image is not of a Viking warrior but a Christian ruler. In the pages of the New Minster *Liber Vitae*, Cnut and his queen are depicted presenting a massive gold cross to the community (see picture 1). The simplicity of the line drawing, which shows the king as a mature man in his thirties, is striking; face and body are conveyed in a manner recalling the strong outlines and dynamic detail of Hergé's drawings of Tintin. In the 1980s, academics from the Danish National Museum found inspiration in the manuscript folio for their recreation of a Viking ruler (see picture 14). Their attention to detail – using a model clad in garments based on ones found in a high-status grave at Mammen and sporting a rather dashing beard – went some way to converting the New Minster's rendering of Cnut into what a modern audience might expect of a Viking king. But a model's grim expression and authentic attire could only go so far. If we disregard the fact that Cnut was first and foremost a Viking warrior, it is difficult to think of either the medieval manuscript or modern photograph simply as images of a Viking king. That may have been precisely what the New Minster artist intended.

Cnut's beard, for example, is not that of a 'Viking' in the

way that a 'Dane' or a 'pagan' might have been determined as 'other' in the late Anglo-Saxon period. By the eleventh century, the fashion of so-called 'Vikings' may have been a close shave on both the face and the back of the head.[6] Indeed, the nickname of Swein 'Forkbeard', if it were contemporary, may have been intended to evoke the beards of the Old Testament rulers in Anglo-Saxon manuscripts from around this period, which were sometimes bifurcated, as we see in the contemporary depiction of Pharaoh in the *Old English Hexateuch* (see picture 7). In the same way, the New Minster picture of Cnut was intended to invoke the wisdom and authority of a Christian ruler. He was evidently in his early or mid thirties at this point and thus was the age of Æthelred's father, King Edgar, at the time of his second, highly imperial, coronation in 973. Edgar is presented as bearded in another New Minster manuscript, the so-called 'Golden Charter' of 966, which probably provided the model of a hairy-faced Christian king for Cnut's New Minster depiction.[7] There were good reasons for this, rooted in contemporary notions of Christian kingship. In 1018 and 1019, Cnut, at the suggestion of his advisers, most likely the veteran statesman Archbishop Wulfstan, recalled the kingship of Edgar in his legal proclamations.[8] In 1031, Cnut was older, probably wiser and certainly more experienced. The crown worn by him is an indication that the artist and perhaps Cnut himself understood the power of an imperial message. Edgar had not worn such a crown but Cnut, who had been to the imperial coronation of Conrad, is depicted on the *Liber Vitae* image as wearing a crown like that worn by the Holy Roman Emperor.

We have already seen the power and authority exercised by Emma as an English queen, and the image is in many ways just as much a depiction of her queenship as it is of Cnut's kingship,[9] but the illustration in the New Minster *Liber Vitae* conveys as a whole what made Cnut tick as an English ruler. The positioning of two pairs of hands in the picture serves to highlight the most important aspects of his rule. The king's right hand is on the cross that he and his wife are depicted as presenting to the minster, precisely at the place where the feet of Christ would otherwise be. Whether the artist really thought of Cnut as a latter-day Mary Magdalene is open to debate: Emma's position in the image is in that traditionally reserved for Mary, mother of God; Mary Magdalene is usually her counterpart. What is important is that the two royal figures bear witness to the risen Christ depicted in majesty at the top of the image. Cnut's left hand, meanwhile, rests on the hilt of a sword projecting out of the frame, perhaps reminding viewers of the fact that his rulership of the kingdom stemmed from conquest.[10] If that impression is what was intended, a second pair of hands and set of gestures form a stark reminder of the source of royal power and an indication that the conquest was legitimate – the angel whose left hand sets upon Cnut's head the (imperial) crown of authority points with his right hand to Christ, whose ultimate majesty had to be acknowledged by an earthly ruler.

But if we imagine turning the folio, as few now have the privilege to do, we come face to face with what the notion of salvation meant to the New Minster's community (see picture 2). A two-page spread depicts the monastic community and perhaps the wider English people, the *Angelcynn*, as they await their doom, with the despatch of the unrighteous to Hell and the salvation of the righteous. Overleaf from Cnut and Emma, the link between the king, the community of the righteous and the gates to Heaven is made clear. One of the figures awaiting his turn among the community may be a representation of Cnut himself after his death, devoid of his crown, his hair slightly longer, but the beard distinctly that of the king, and holding a palm of victory to represent the resurrection to come (Emma presumably had to look elsewhere for a comparable image as she could not be a lay member of a male religious community). As the monks of the New Minster opened this book in their daily service to pray for those of the community who had died, during Cnut's lifetime and after, they would have seen the depiction of the king and his wife, and looked at the very cross that he had presented, perhaps acquired in Rome itself. And perhaps Cnut too felt that sense of being part of that important Christian community at the heart of his kingdom.[11]

Ecclesiastical patronage was a means of binding the king ever closer to his family, both the living and the dead. The fictive brotherhood with Cnut's immediate predecessor, Edmund Ironside, was increasingly drawn upon later in Cnut's reign. Edmund had been buried at Glastonbury but recent work on the royal burials in Winchester Cathedral suggests that at some point after a visit to Glastonbury in November 1032, the anniversary of Edmund's death, Cnut had Edmund's body – or some of his remains – brought from Glastonbury to the Old Minster in Winchester in a plan to develop the Old Minster as a royal burial house for

1. Cnut with Emma, presenting a gold cross to the New
Minster, Winchester, as depicted in the frontispiece of the
New Minster *Liber Vitae* ('Book of Life', 1031).

2. A figure looking remarkably like Cnut (far left) among the community of the righteous about to enter Heaven on the verso of the frontispiece of the New Minster *Liber Vitae*.

3. A coin of Cnut, with the obverse depicting the king as a warrior, complete with helmet, from *c.* 1024–30. The military message projected by this sort of coin may relate to a time when Cnut was fighting for control of a developing Scandinavian realm.

4. Early-modern bone chest in Winchester Cathedral said to contain the bones of King Cnut alongside those of other West Saxon notables.

5. Cnut (depicted with a Viking ship on his shield) and his opponent King Edmund Ironside in single combat, as imagined in the thirteenth century by Matthew Paris in his *Chronica Majora*.

6. Queen Emma receives her *Encomium Emmae Reginae* (*c.* 1041), presumably from its author, as depicted in the book's frontispiece. The figures on the right are thought to be her sons Harthacnut and Edward.

7. Pharaoh as a wise Anglo-Saxon ruler surrounded by his witan, as depicted by the Canterbury artist of the *Old English Hexateuch* in the eleventh century. The artist may have had Cnut or Æthelred in mind.

8. The minster church at Deerhurst (Gloucestershire), near to 'Ola's Island' (Olney), where a peace treaty was agreed between Edmund Ironside and Cnut in autumn 1016.

9. The Jelling Runestone (Jutland, Denmark), erected by Cnut's grandfather Harald Bluetooth, probably in the 960s, declares that Harald 'won for himself all of Denmark and Norway and made the Danes Christian'.

10. 'Roskilde 6', a warship from Cnut's time found in 1997 at the site of the Danish Viking Ship Museum in Roskilde (here on temporary display at the British Museum).

11. A charter of Cnut, recorded in the witness list as 'King of the English', granting an estate at Drayton (Hampshire) to the community of the New Minster, Winchester, in Easter 1019.

13. A thirteenth-century depiction from the altarpiece at Trondheim Cathedral, Norway, of Cnut's Norwegian opponent King (later Saint) Olaf.

12. The 'Winchester Frieze', found in excavations of the site of Old Minster, Winchester, has been plausibly suggested as depicting a scene from the Old Norse *Völsunga Saga*.

14. A modern recreation of a Viking ruler for Denmark's National Museum, based on the depiction of Cnut in the New Minster *Liber Vitae* and on clothes found at a grave in Mammen, Denmark.

15. This painting by James McConnell is one of many modern representations of 'Canute' attempting to order the tide to turn, inspired by the account of the twelfth-century historian Henry of Huntingdon.

Cnut's dynasty.[12] Moving important remains to another site was not unprecedented in Anglo-Saxon England. Winchester's churches periodically received them and the translation of the martyred archbishop Saint Ælfheah from London to Canterbury was part of Cnut's early Christian policy. Kings' bodies were included among these.[13] In the ninth century, Alfred had had his father moved to Winchester, and Alfred's body was itself moved (albeit only by a few feet to the neighbouring church) shortly after his death. During Æthelred's reign, meanwhile, the body of the king's murdered brother, Edward, was ferried back and forth across Wessex.

What had determined such a move for Edmund? His posthumous presence in the English kingdom may be linked to Cnut's policy. Cnut was clearly not hostile to Edmund himself. He had declared at Oxford in 1018 to be following in the footsteps of King Edgar, the grandfather of Edmund, who was the only other later king buried at Glastonbury. Moreover, Edmund's 'Ironside' nickname was shared with a semi-legendary ninth-century Viking, Bjorn Járnsíða. Given that Edmund's nickname is first recorded in 1057, it is likely to be a post-mortem coinage, but it is significant even so, as it may reflect the increasing importance of Edmund to Cnut. Edmund's prominence in the Anglo-Saxon Chronicle as a valiant opponent and later as Cnut's 'sworn brother' might attest to this recasting of their relationship if we consider the Chronicle as a version of history linked to Cnut's court.[14]

Cnut evidently became yet more confident and continued to flex his muscles throughout his reign in England as he did abroad through the 1020s and 1030s. His emergence as a fully fledged member of the West Saxon royal kin reflects this. But if Cnut's evident embracing of his adopted royal family can be linked to anything specific, it is to the phases of potential opposition that might come from inside his English kingdom and from overseas. In that sense, Cnut's family policy was reactive but it was also part of a developing political game of action and reaction. The threatened invasion from Normandy by the surviving sons of King Æthelred in 1033 or 1034 is relevant here. If Cnut's *own* heir, Harthacnut, was in Denmark and another son, Swein, born to Ælfgifu of Northampton, was busy asserting his own position in Norway against increasing opposition, Cnut's reference to the familial memory of Edmund was particularly judicious. It helped to bolster the king's position in England at a time when there were problems apparent not only in Norway but also threatening Cnut directly in the form of the heirs of Æthelred in Normandy. Ultimately, as a legitimate king in a kingdom favoured by God, with links to sainted family members, Cnut had found himself with a good hand to play and he was obliged to play it. That link to the Christian ideology of English rulership provided him with a major part of his identity as an English king.

This policy can be seen in Cnut's links to other West Saxon royal foundations and royal family members. He appears to have embraced the cult of King Edward 'the Martyr', murdered by associates of his half-brother Æthelred in 978 and resting at Shaftesbury Abbey by the time of Cnut's reign. The story of Edward's death might have been useful to Cnut because it portrayed Æthelred's succession

to Edward in a negative light.[15] After all, the killing of
God's anointed king in 978 would have helped make
Cnut's kingship appear part of the divinely directed narrative of conquest championed by Wulfstan, and, conveniently
for Cnut, this would have had a knock-on effect on how
Æthelred's heirs were perceived. Equally, stories developing in the eleventh century of the involvement of Æthelred's
mother, Queen Ælfthryth, in Saint Edward's murder might
not have been unwelcome to Queen Emma, either. However, there was a sense of continuity too: Æthelred had
also patronized his half-brother,[16] so Cnut's veneration of
Saint Edward may simply have been less a specific policy
than part of the way in which he linked himself to a family
network of royal dead.

Cnut also appeared to tap into the cult of Æthelred's sister, Saint Edith, which had been developing around the
same time as that of Edward.[17] A story from a later period
has a sceptical Cnut ordering Edith's tomb at Wilton Abbey
to be opened to see whether the body was incorrupt because
he did not believe that the daughter of so lascivious a king as
Edgar could be a saint. This may owe more to twelfth-
century gossip than to the patterns of patronage of Cnut's
own day (the doubting Cnut was, of course, proved
wrong!),[18] but we might be more confident of an insight into
the perils of North Sea kingship provided by the record of
Cnut's invocation of Edith while at sea during a storm.
Upon his safe return, the king ordered a shrine to be built to
her. In the late eleventh century, Edith's hagiographer, Goscelin of Saint-Bertin, recorded that though Cnut's generosity
had been 'overflowing', the shrine had 'thin gilding', and the

workmen who made it were later struck blind by divine ret-
ribution.[19] Though Goscelin's stories may go over the top in
the sanctification of their subjects and stock use of miracles
(this wasn't the only time Cnut is said to have promised
something during a storm at sea), a link between Cnut and
Saint Edith at Wilton is likely, particularly as Queen Emma
was also remembered as a patron of the nunnery there.[20]
Knowledge at Wilton that Cnut regularly went overseas
might quickly transform into a miraculous story. Commu-
nities remembered shrines, as indeed they remembered
donations of valuable crosses, and the shrine of Saint Edith
might still even have been present in the church some eight
decades after its commission by Cnut.

But the expression of belief and memory took many
forms in Cnut's English kingdom. Back in Winchester,
only a few yards from the New Minster, where the *Liber
Vitae* lay on the high altar, was an object which now seems
to us to belong to a very different world from shrines and
great crosses. The only block found so far of what has been
dubbed the 'Winchester Frieze' is a 70cm-high piece of
Bath stone, thought to illustrate an episode in the *Völsunga
Saga* in which the hero Sigmund (better known as Sieg-
mund in Wagner's *Ring Cycle*) frees himself from captivity
by entrapping a wolf that comes to eat him and his com-
panions. Depicting part of a man's body – a bound head
and hands – and a wolf-like animal, the stone has been
placed squarely in the context of northern European pagan
tradition.[21] (See picture 12.)

In this respect, it may seem surprising that it should be
displayed in the Old Minster, a church that was, as a royal

cathedral, perhaps the foremost at this time in the English kingdom. Assuming that this interpretation is right, why would a pagan image be placed on view, at the east end of the church, close to royal tombs? The message of unity that it projects is essential to understanding the North Sea outlook of Cnut's rule. The story that it portrays links the Danish and West Saxon royal houses in a way that a biblical narrative could not. However, the identification with the *Völsunga Saga* is not uncontroversial. Some modern commentators, dating the carving to later in the eleventh century, have suggested that it is in fact inspired by classical history[22] but such confusion may not have been felt by a contemporary audience, who would not have been perturbed by any blurring of boundaries between apparently contradictory thought-worlds. For Cnut's court and for a Christian audience in the eleventh century, stories such as that of Sigmund could be used as part of a historical tradition, just as the Old Testament and ancient world were part of the historical past. They helped to inform the audience as to the place of the rulers in their present.

This argument has been extended in recent decades to the *Beowulf* manuscript, normally regarded as the oldest surviving epic poem in the English language. The *Beowulf* poem tells of a hero of the Geats, a tribe from modern-day Sweden, who serves with the Danes to rid them of a terrible monster, centuries before the reign of Cnut, in the so-called 'Migration Period' of the fifth and sixth centuries. Many elements of the story are indeed of great antiquity and its place in the history of English literature is not in doubt, but the manuscript itself was written at some point around the beginning of the eleventh century. Arguments have been made proposing that the composition of the poem in its current form is actually close to the date of the manuscript itself. Of course, within that frame there is debate as to whether the manuscript was composed in Æthelred's time or in Cnut's reign.[23] If the *Beowulf* manuscript were written for an audience associated with Cnut's court, the Scandinavian past told in an Anglo-Saxon story makes a great deal of sense. If written in the run-up to the great conquest of 1016, however, the themes of the loss of a great and noble house, the passing of ages and the fates of men were hardly a world away from the sentiments of the likes of Wulfstan, either. Those themes and that ability of an Anglo-Saxon audience to engage with a Scandinavian history help us to understand just how a Danish ruler, a latter-day member of the dynasty in the *Beowulf* story, the Scyldings, could be on the throne in England for almost two decades.

So references to the old pagan world in England did not mean that Cnut was 'half Christian' or a secret pagan, or that members of his court held such sentiments. Instead, such traditions were valuable for the Anglo-Danish kingship, just as Charlemagne, otherwise a figure linked with Christian reform who destroyed pagan shrines in Germany, could also be remembered for learning the 'old' Frankish 'songs', or Christian writers in twelfth- and thirteenth-century Iceland could readily reframe the pagan mythologies of their ancestors. It did not make them pagans but, rather, showed their confidence in Christianity. This is also reflected in the poetry of the skalds at Cnut's court, who freely mixed pagan and Christian imagery, in comparison to the skalds of Olaf Haraldsson, who were careful to make reference only to Christianity.[24] Olaf was a first-generation convert to Christianity whose faith had to be emphasized to contrast him with his predecessor, Olaf Tryggvasson, also a first-generation convert, but from a different dynasty. Cnut was evidently more secure, at least in England, and though he would not attain the sainthood of Olaf Haraldsson after his death, his piety could be expressed in different ways. Such references to the pre-Christian past as the story of Sigmund at the Old Minster could be subtle, like the burial at one of the Winchester Minster cemeteries of one 'Huskarl', a man who saw himself as part of an eleventh-century Scandinavian affinity whose name and/or title was memorialized in runes.[25] Though used in a Christian setting, in the form of a once-pagan medium, they were reaching back to a different part of a shared past and enhanced rule across the North Sea. Such messages also had much in common with the celebration of the cults of members of Cnut's Christian royal family. They all stemmed from the same set of desires: a wish to learn about the past and link oneself with it in order to enhance one's own prestige.

Casting Cnut himself as a neophyte, a new convert, might explain the apparently easy use of paganism and traditional readings of Cnut linked with Swein's supposed pagan rebellion against Harald Bluetooth in late tenth-century Denmark. However, once we recognize that Adam of Bremen, the main late eleventh-century source of the stories of Swein Forkbeard's paganism, had a vested interest in showing the recent, apparently shallow roots of Danish

Christianity (so justifying the subjection of Danish Christians to the authority of Hamburg-Bremen), Cnut's Christian upbringing seems less unlikely. One version of Adam of Bremen's *History* does in fact record Cnut's receipt of a baptismal name, Lambert, 'having put aside his pagan name'.[26] 'Lambert' is also recorded as a 'most pious king' in an Exeter list of deaths for 11 November, close enough to Cnut's date of death of 12 November for it to be significant.[27] Given the 'pagan' connotations of Cnut's name, it is not impossible that, like seventh-century Anglo-Saxon rulers who converted to Christianity, keeping one or more of their children unbaptized while they thought through the implications of the new faith,[28] Swein may have delayed the baptism of his younger son, with the result that Cnut was given a different baptismal name. At the same time, although different baptismal names are not uncommon, a Christian king sharing his name with an earlier pagan Viking king at this period does not seem to have been an issue, particularly as the name 'Cnut' harked back to an older Danish dynasty. The choice of 'Lambert', on the other hand, may have linked Cnut to his mother's Piast dynasty, also recently Christian, in Poland.[29] That Saint Lambert was martyred because he denounced the irregularity of a Frankish king's marriage would have been particularly ironic to Adam of Bremen, who elsewhere noted the birth of certain of Cnut's children to a 'concubine'.[30] That fact, and the record of Swein's exile of his wife, Cnut's mother, at some point during Cnut's childhood, may be why references to him as 'Lambert' are so rare.

Whatever lay behind the names, though, Cnut was

capable of grand gestures of Christian piety. It is all too easy to be sceptical about motives when looking at the bigamous imperialist through twenty-first-century eyes. In the eleventh century, religious actions *were* acts of policy (Wulfstan even adapted an Æthelredian text, the *Institutes of Polity*, to convey that message in Cnut's reign). In June 1023, perhaps at the height of Cnut and Thorkell's rivalry, the relics of Saint Ælfheah were translated from St Paul's in London, near where Ælfheah had died in 1012, back to Canterbury, where Ælfheah had been archbishop. The assertion of the interests of Æthelnoth, the newly invested Archbishop of Canterbury, a figure later linked with the appointment of English bishops in Scandinavia, is likely to have played a role in the translation.[31] According to later accounts, it did not happen unopposed, and Cnut had to deploy a force of housecarls to prevent the Londoners from keeping a saint they had regarded as their own for the past ten years. It would not be surprising if such accounts were true for Cnut's hostility to London, which had been taxed heavily in 1018, and his apparent preference for Winchester as a political centre would suggest that this was a religious policy rooted in an eleventh-century political reality.[32]

Cnut visited many religious houses in England during his reign. This was, of course, what early medieval kings had to do in order demonstrate that they were in control, but for Cnut there is more than a whiff of political theatre, of spectacle, to his religious visits. Not least among these is his visit to Durham and a five-mile barefoot pilgrimage to the shrine of Saint Cuthbert there, which seems to have occurred at a political high point in 1031.[33] Cnut would go on to receive the submission of Scottish rulers, a matter that met specific strategic needs, as we have seen, but in a world where gestures, symbolism and the performance of pious actions had deep meaning, the monastic community of Durham may have now been willing to overlook, at least for the moment, the killing of the Northumbrian Earl Uhtred around the start of Cnut's career.

Cnut died in Shaftesbury in November 1035 at about forty years of age. We don't know why he died there or what he was doing at the time. Analysis of royal bones, which include those of Cnut, in Winchester Cathedral may yet tell us a great deal, perhaps even the cause of death, but we can be pretty sure that he did not die a heroic death in battle or even in some minor skirmish. For one thing, given the number of churches that could boast of links to Cnut and the contemporary need in Scandinavia for royal saints, had he met a violent death, like Olaf or indeed Cnut's later namesake, Saint Cnut (d. 1085), it is likely that his cult would have been swept up with suitable saintly vigour. We will not, alas, be able to find out whether thoughts of salvation were in his mind when Cnut's final moments came. In Shaftesbury he was near to, if not in the presence of, a royal saint, Edward the Martyr. Given Cnut's displays of solicitousness to many members of his adopted family, and the way in which he drew himself closer to them, particularly as he grew older, it is worth wondering whether he would have expected Saint Edward to come to his aid as he breathed his last.

6

The End of Danish England

For a king with such strong maritime associations, the relatively static nature of Cnut's final years may seem surprising.
He was in Rome in 1027 and travelled to Norway with a
great fleet in 1028, returning to England the following year.
He travelled to Scotland in 1031 but after that he seems to
have remained in England. The evidence of cultural investment in Winchester suggests that, by and large, he spent
much time there.[1] Known excursions at this period are
Cnut's visit to the grave of Edmund in Glastonbury in 1032,
a trip to Northumbria in 1033 recorded in a York Minster
charter[2] and his visit to Shaftesbury at the time of his death
in 1035. It is unlikely that Cnut travelled again to Rome, as
was once generally thought, based on the misdating of the
journey in 1027 to 1031 by the *Anglo-Saxon Chronicle*.
There are echoes here of the last years of Charlemagne, who
remained in Aachen for much of his final decade. Charlemagne was much older than Cnut when he died, but getting
subordinates to travel to you, rather than the other way
round, has always been a way of showing superiority.[3] There
is a certain paradox here, according to recent work on the
skaldic poets at Cnut's court: these poets extolled the virtues
of his Viking career, particularly his Norwegian conquests,

but they mostly plied their trade at the point at which he was least like a Viking. Before then, Cnut had thrown Danish and English weight around in the Baltic in the early 1020s, asserted Danish authority over the Norwegians by 1028 and had done his damnedest to assert himself over the Swedes in 1026–7 – matters that help with the dating of these skaldic poems[4] – but the absence of Cnut from the famous Norwegian Battle of Stiklestad (1030), which played a significant role in securing his Norwegian realm, is striking. One version of the *Anglo-Saxon Chronicle* presents it as a killing of King Olaf 'by the people gathered against him'.[5] By and large, it was a local conflict and perhaps events had moved too quickly for Cnut to react. However, given the killing of the rebel King Olaf, and the reimposition of Danish over-lordship on Norway through Cnut's family, it is none the less odd that Cnut was not involved in Norwegian affairs directly, as he had been in 1028.

Of course, we don't know what Cnut intended in November 1035 beyond going to Shaftesbury. Perhaps he planned to cross the North Sea again once the winter had passed, but there are hints of an illness that, while lingering, eventually proved fatal. Harald Harefoot, Cnut's son by his first wife, Ælfgifu of Northampton, was in England to contest the kingdom just after his father's death and the *Anglo-Saxon Chronicle* reports that *lithsmen* ('fleetmen' or ships' crews) in London gave him their support.[6] Though these men might have been in London for some time before 1035, it is feasible that Harald would have heard of his father's illness, bringing a fleet to demonstrate that he was a worthy successor. The Norman author William of Jumièges also refers to

Cnut, in ill health, offering half his kingdom to the sons of Æthelred the Unready.[7] Though that offer should be read with more than a pinch of salt, the timing of the abortive attack by the Normans implies that Cnut's inactivity in his final years had not gone unnoticed by contemporaries. Had the illness that is likely to have eventually killed him manifested itself much earlier than 1035, it could have meant that Cnut was unable to make the sea journeys that had given him such glory in his youth and early adulthood. If so, the skaldic praises about the Old North and a Viking way of life might have taken on a bittersweet quality when recited in the green and pleasant valleys of Wessex.

> Shaker of the sword-belt's ice, you let the prow of the tough steed of the girdle of all lands turn west into the sea.[8]

Still, such words were a verbal reminder of the sheer achievement of the empire built by a man who was scarcely older when he died than Duke William of Normandy at the time of his conquest of England in 1066.

Those comparisons with William – 'the Conqueror' – are important here. It is sometimes said that the Danish conquest of England in 1016 was of little lasting significance because Cnut established neither a dynasty nor an empire with any continuity.[9] His two surviving sons, both born of different mothers (Harald Harefoot and Harthacnut), drew their rivalries into the open in contests that emerged in the wake of his death and which brought out more demonstrations of Norman support for the sons of Æthelred. Harald reigned for only five years, ruling alone for only the last three of these. Only two years after coming to the throne, with Æthelred's son Edward the Confessor waiting in the wings, Harthacnut died suddenly in 1042. William, by contrast, apparently established a dynasty that stretched to this day. Of course, there is some merit to this argument. For much of the Middle Ages the legitimacy of English kings was based on the right to rule both England *and* Normandy, with other chunks of France: a very different axis from the North Sea world.

But the newly minted Anglo-Norman realm suffered two decades of uncertainty following the Conqueror's death in 1087, as sons squabbled for their cross-Channel possessions. It was not surprising that Cnut's North Sea empire did not go quietly, either. It is testimony to the impact of his reign, in just the same manner as the aftermath of the death of William I, that Cnut's control of the English kingdom for nearly nineteen years and the rule by his sons for a further seven did much to determine the shape of the English polity inherited by Edward the Confessor in 1042. Edward was unable to step in where his father had left off in 1016. The longer-term significance of Cnut's reign is that, within living memory at the time of the conquest of 1066, a conqueror had taken control of the English kingdom in 1016, determining the claims of both Harold Godwinesson, linked by marriage to Cnut's royal family, and Harald 'Hardrada' of Norway, who claimed England through an agreement with Harthacnut. Furthermore, the networks of relationships established by an Anglo-Danish aristocracy during the course of two generations under Cnut and his sons, and which Edward had tried hard to deal with, had to be dismantled in the wake of the 1066 conquest in a manner that contrasts with the relative continuity after 1016.

Of course, any assessment of Cnut's reign needs considering not just in terms of his legacy but in his own ability to rule. During his career we see him shifting to meet threats from different quarters across a wide realm. In 1015 and 1016, he looked to be the king in the North, a Viking warlord successor to his father. In 1017–19, when circumstances changed and when English æthelings were a clear and present danger (while Cnut had no English sons himself for part of this period), he became the English king. From 1019 we see a Danish king who utilized a redefined message of Englishness, reshaped and linked through the use of the shared network across the North Sea between an English kingdom and a changing Scandinavian world. After 1026, his Scandinavian experience was determined by the Battle of Holy River, in which we see a developing imperial policy that traversed the North Sea. Also around this time, perhaps in response to a renewed threat from Normandy, we see redoubled efforts to establish legitimacy in the south of England.

This need to reshape and adapt to circumstances was the result of a political world that depended upon the king's personal connections for it to function. As a result, it could falter if he did not move rapidly and decisively. Cnut's ruthlessness appears as a stark reminder of how a particular type of early medieval ruler might be expected to behave, especially when faced with the inevitable bouts of treachery that rule on such a scale might be expected to engender. In this light, Cnut's actions may have been bloody but they were never bloodthirsty. In the wake of the Norman Conquest of 1066, a skaldic poet, Thorkell Skallason, declared: 'it is true that the killing in England will be a long time ending'.[10] Such words were unlikely to be heard in Cnut's England. Although his Norwegian foes lamented his empire-building because it brought the harshness of the regime of Ælfgifu and Swein, at each stage in England, and indeed in Denmark, royal violence seems to have been episodic, intended chiefly as a demonstration of power. Typified by the mutilation of hostages at the start of Cnut's career in England, his use of violence was ugly, brutal and created long-lasting pain, but it made a point. Above all, it ended quickly. It is perhaps no surprise that while there is little doubt that Cnut was responsible for killing or ordering the deaths of nobles and royals who threatened his rule, particularly in 1017 in England and around 1026–7 in Denmark, other accounts of politically motivated deaths, particularly those of Edmund Ironside and Jarl Håkon, are only attributed to him much later. That they exist, however, is not just evidence of later storytelling but of the fact that Cnut had acted with brutal violence when the occasion did demand it. A reputation as a ruthless ruler that would last beyond his lifetime was sealed. In that respect, at least, Cnut had succeeded.

Notes

Where possible, references are to English translations of primary sources, though quotations have sometimes been adjusted for clarity if needed.

ABBREVIATIONS

Adam	Adam of Bremen, *History of the Archbishops of Hamburg-Bremen*, trans. Francis J. Tschan (New York: Columbia University Press, 1959)
'Æthelings'	Simon Keynes, 'The Æthelings in Normandy', *Anglo-Norman Studies*, 13 (1991)
ASC	*Anglo-Saxon Chronicle*, ed. Dorothy Whitelock, David C. Douglas and Susie I. Tucker, rev. edn (London: Eyre and Spottiswoode, 1965) [a useful translation lining up different versions ('A' through to 'F') on the page]
'Burial of Æthelred'	Simon Keynes, 'The Burial of King Æthelred the Unready at St Paul's', in *The English and their Legacy 900–1200*, ed. David Roffe (Woodbridge: Boydell Press, 2012)
Danes in Wessex	*Danes in Wessex: The Scandinavian Impact on Southern England, c.800–c.1100*, ed. Ryan Lavelle and Simon Roffey (Oxford: Oxbow, 2016)
EHD	*English Historical Documents: Volume I: c.500–1042*, ed. Dorothy Whitelock, 2nd edn (London: Methuen, 1979)
Empire of Cnut	Timothy Bolton, *The Empire of Cnut the Great* (Leiden: Brill, 2009)
Encomium	*Encomium Emmae Reginae*, ed. A. Campbell (London: Royal Historical Society, 1949)
Hearne	*Hemingi Chartularium Ecclesiæ Wigorniensis*, ed. T. Hearne, 2 vols (Oxford: 1723)
Insley	Charles Insley, 'Politics, Conflict and Kinship in Early Eleventh-Century Mercia', *Midland History*, 25 (2000)
JW	John of Worcester, *The Chronicle of John of Worcester: Volume II: The Annals from 450–1066*, ed. R. R. Darlington and P. McGurk (Oxford: Oxford University Press, 1995)
Lawson, *Cnut*	M. K. Lawson, *Cnut: England's Viking King* (Stroud: Tempus, 2004)
Queen Emma	Pauline Stafford, *Queen Emma and Queen Edith: Queenship and Women's Power in Eleventh-Century England* (Oxford: Blackwell, 1997)

Ridyard	Susan Ridyard, *The Royal Saints of Anglo-Saxon England* (Cambridge: Cambridge University Press, 1988)
Rumble	*The Reign of Cnut*, ed. Alexander Rumble (London: Leicester University Press, 1994)
S	*Anglo-Saxon Charters: An Annotated List and Bibliography*, ed. P. H. Sawyer (London: Royal Historical Society, 1968) [online at www.esawyer.org.uk]
Thietmar	Thietmar, in *Ottonian Germany: The Chronicon of Thietmar of Merseburg*, trans. David A. Warner (Manchester: Manchester University Press, 2001)
Wormald	Patrick Wormald, *The Making of English Law: King Alfred to the Twelfth Century: Volume I: Legislation and its Limits* (Oxford: Blackwell, 1999)

NOTE ON THE TEXT

1. The *Encomium Emmae Reginae*, written around 1041, is used in this study (see edition details in 'Abbreviations' above) rather than the recently rediscovered post-1042 text acquired by the Royal Library, Copenhagen.
2. *Knytlinga Saga*, in *The Viking Age: A Reader*, ed. Angus A. Somerville and R. Andrew McDonald (Toronto: Toronto University Press, 2010), p. 456.

I. CNUT THE CONQUEROR

1. Henry of Huntingdon, *Historia Anglorum: The History of the English People*, ed. Diana Greenway (Oxford: Oxford University Press, 1996), pp. 367–9.
2. Ibid., pp. 368–9.
3. Emily Winkler, *Royal Responsibility in Anglo-Norman Narratives* (Oxford: Oxford University Press, 2017).
4. A useful example is Hallvarðr Háreksblesi, *Knútsdrápa*, trans. Roberta Frank, 'King Cnut in the Verse of his Skalds', in Rumble, pp. 119–21.
5. A certain 'Wrytsleof', perhaps a rendering of the name Vratislav, who may have been a Slavic visitor to Cnut's court linked with Cnut's mother's side of the family, is recorded in a Winchester charter of 1026 (S 962). See *Empire of Cnut*, p. 216.
6. Details of the ship, acknowledging the uncertainty as to who ordered its construction, are summarized in Jan Bill, 'Roskilde 6', in *Vikings: Life and Legend*, ed. Gareth Williams, Peter Pentz and Matthias Wemhoff (London: British Museum Press, 2014), pp. 228–33.
7. Klaus van Eickels, 'Gendered Violence: Castration and Blinding as Punishment for Treason in Normandy and Anglo-Norman England', *Gender and History*, 16.3 (2004), pp. 588–602.
8. Alice Hicklin, 'The Role of Hostages in the Danish Conquests of England and Norway, 1013–30', in *Medieval Hostageship c.700–c.1500*, ed. Katherine Weikert and Matthew Bennett (London: Routledge, 2016), pp. 60–78.
9. Hearne, I, pp. 259–60.

10. Louise Loe, Angela Boyle, Helen Webb and David Score, *'Given to the Ground': A Viking Age Mass Grave on Ridgeway Hill, Weymouth* (Dorchester: Oxford Archaeology, 2014), pp. 13–15 and 224–8.

11. Anne Pedersen, 'Monumental Expression and Fortification in Denmark in the Time of King Harald Bluetooth', in *Fortified Settlements in Early Medieval Europe*, ed. Neil Christie and Hajnalka Herold (Oxford: Oxbow, 2016), pp. 68–81.

12. *Encomium*, II.2, pp. 16–17. Niels Lund argues Harald's seniority in 'Cnut's Danish Kingdom', in Rumble, p. 28.

13. Lund, 'Cnut's Danish Kingdom', pp. 27–8. For Swein's first liaison, see Peter Sawyer, 'Swein Forkbeard and the Historians', in *Church and Chronicle in the Middle Ages*, ed. Ian Wood and G. A. Loud (London: Hambledon, 1991), pp. 27–40.

14. *Knytlinga Saga*, p. 445.

15. Sawyer, 'Swein Forkbeard and the Historians', pp. 38–40.

16. Durham *Liber Vitae*, British Library, MS Cotton Domitian A.vii, fol. 15v (online at http://www.bl.uk/manuscripts/Viewer.aspx?ref=cotton_ms_domitian_a_vii_fs001r).

17. *ASC* 1013. See editorial comments by Campbell in *Encomium*, pp. liii and lxiii.

18. Insley, pp. 28–42.

19. This misinterpretation is explored by Timothy Bolton, 'Ælfgifu of Northampton: Cnut the Great's "Other Woman"', *Nottingham Medieval Studies*, 51 (2007), pp. 247–68.

20. *Encomium*, I.5, pp. 14–15.

21. Herman's *Life of St Edmund*, chs 4–9, ed. Tom Licence, *Miracles of St Edmund* (Oxford: Oxford University Press, 2014), pp. 14–25.

22. See Malcolm Godden, 'Apocalypse and Invasion in Late Anglo-Saxon England', in *From Anglo-Saxon to Early Middle English*, ed. Douglas Gray, Malcolm Godden and T. F. Hoad (Oxford: Clarendon Press, 1994), pp. 137–40.

23. Jonathan Wilcox, 'Wulfstan's *Sermo Lupi ad Anglos* as Political Performance: 16 February 1014 and Beyond', in *Wulfstan, Archbishop of York*, ed. Matthew Townend (Turnhout: Brepols, 2004), pp. 375–96.

24. *ASC* CDE 1014; Pauline Stafford, 'The Laws of Cnut and the History of Anglo-Saxon Royal Promises', *Anglo-Saxon England*, 10 (1981), pp. 173–90.

25. *EHD*, pp. 929–34.

26. Ann Williams, 'Some Notes and Considerations on Problems Connected with the English Royal Succession, 860–1066', *Anglo-Norman Studies*, 1 (1979), pp. 144–67, 225–33.

27. *ASC* CDE 1014.

28. On the jarls of Skåne, see *Empire of Cnut*, pp. 203–20. The detail of fosterage (whereby families brought up each other's children for the benefit of political relationships) in one version of the *Jomsviking Saga* is dismissed by Campbell (*Encomium*, p. 89).

29. *Encomium*, II.3, pp. 18–19. See Ann Williams, 'Thorkell the Tall and the Bubble Reputation: The Vicissitudes of Fame', in *Danes in Wessex*, pp. 149–50.

30. *ASC* CDE 1012–14.

31. *Empire of Cnut*, pp. 155–6.

32. Thietmar, VII.40, p. 335; *Encomium*, II.4, pp. 20–21; Lund, 'Cnut's Danish Kingdom', p. 29.

33. *ASC* 1015; Insley, pp. 33–4.

34. *Encomium*, II.5, pp. 20–21. See David Hill, 'An Urban Policy for Cnut?', in Rumble, pp. 101–5.

35. *ASC* CDE 1009.

36. *ASC* CDE 1015.

37. C. J. Morris, *Marriage and Murder in Eleventh-Century Northumbria: A Study of 'De Obsessione Dunelmi'* (York: Borthwick Institute, 1992), p. 3.

38. *ASC* CDE 1016.

39. A useful recent assessment of the evidence is Alex Woolf, *From Pictland to Alba: 789–1070* (Edinburgh: Edinburgh University Press, 2007), pp. 236–40.

40. Evidence for the presence of the body in York prior to burial, probably at Lund, is addressed by Martin Biddle and Birthe Kjølbye-Biddle, 'Danish Royal Burials in Winchester: Cnut and his Family', in *Danes in Wessex*, pp. 234–5. *Encomium*, II.3, pp. 18–19, implies that Swein's body went straight to Denmark.

41. *ASC* CDE 1016; this is also recorded in a slightly garbled manner in Thietmar, VII.40, p. 335.

42. See 'Burial of Æthelred', pp. 137–42.

43. JW 1016, pp. 484–5.

44. Lawson, *Cnut*, p. 82.

45. Some transitional coins from the time carry Cnut's name while retaining the design of coinage from later in Æthelred's reign. See Kenneth Jonsson, 'The Coinage of Cnut', in Rumble, pp. 197–201.

46. On the location of the battle and difficulties of identification, see Warwick Rodwell, 'The Battle of *Assandun* and its Memorial Church: A Reappraisal', in *The Battle of Maldon: Fiction and Fact*, ed. Janet Cooper (London: Hambledon, 1993), pp. 127–58.

47. *ASC* C 1016.

48. Ryan Lavelle, *Aethelred II: King of the English* (Stroud: History Press, 2008), p. 151. Eadric's nickname is attested in JW 1006, pp. 456–7, and glossed in Latin as 'Acquisitor' in Hearne, I, p. 280; see Insley, pp. 32 and 40, n. 34.

49. *ASC* D 1016.

50. Paul Dalton, 'Sites and Occasions of Peacemaking in England and Normandy, *c. 900–c. 1150*', *Haskins Society Journal*, 16 (2005), p. 14.

51. Ann Williams, *The World Before Domesday: The English Aristocracy, 900–1066* (London: Continuum, 2008), pp. 11–18.

52. Henry of Huntingdon, *Historia Anglorum*, ed. Greenway, pp. 360–61; *Encomium*, II.8, pp. 24–5.

53. The association with a *Holmgangr* (though mistakenly assuming an offer of single combat was made in the Encomiast's account of the Olney meeting, II.13) is discussed by F. E. Wright, *The Cultivation of Saga in Anglo-Saxon England* (Edinburgh: Oliver and Boyd, 1939), pp. 191–6.

54. *ASC* D 1016.

55. Ryan Lavelle, 'Towards a Political Contextualization of Peacemaking and Peace Agreements in Anglo-Saxon England', in *Peace and Negotiation: Strategies for Coexistence in the Middle Ages and the Renaissance*, ed. Diane Wolfthal (Turnhout: Brepols, 2000), pp. 39–55.

56. JW 1016, pp. 492–3 and p. 493, n. 9.

57. *ASC* D 1016.

58. JW 1016, pp. 492–5.

59. 'Æthelings', pp. 177–81 (quotation at p. 181). The fate of Edmund's sons is dealt with by Gabriel Ronay, *The Lost King of England: The East European Adventures of Edward the Exile* (Woodbridge: Boydell Press, 1989).

2. KING OF THE ENGLISH

1. *ASC* CDE 1017.
2. Inge Skovgaard-Petersen, 'The Making of the Danish Kingdom', in *The Cambridge History of Scandinavia*, vol. 1, ed. Knut Helle (Cambridge: Cambridge University Press, 2003), p. 177.
3. Simon Keynes, 'Cnut's Earls', in Rumble, pp. 79–80.
4. Courtnay Konshuh, '*Anraed* in their *Unraed*: The Æthelredian Annals (983–1016) and their Presentation of King and Advisors', *English Studies*, 97.2 (2016), pp. 157–8.
5. Jay Paul Gates, 'A Crowning Achievement: The Royal Execution and Damnation of Eadric Streona', in *Heads Will Roll: Decapitation in the Medieval and Early Modern Imagination*, ed. Larissa Tracy and Jeff Massey (Leiden: Brill, 2012), pp. 53–72.
6. Stephen Baxter, *The Earls of Mercia: Lordship and Power in Late Anglo-Saxon England* (Oxford: Oxford University Press, 2007), pp. 25–31.
7. A 'Beorhtmær' (the name suggesting kinship with Beorhtric) was named in a charter for Eynsham (S 911), an abbey which had benefited from the family of the Æthelweard executed in 1017.
8. Keynes, 'Cnut's Earls', pp. 68–70.
9. For such royal household warriors, see Ryan Lavelle, *Alfred's Wars: Sources and Interpretations of Anglo-Saxon Warfare in the Viking Age* (Woodbridge: Boydell Press, 2010), pp. 107–10.
10. Katharin Mack, 'Changing Thegns: Cnut's Conquest and the English Aristocracy', *Albion*, 16.4 (1984), pp. 375–87.
11. For these debates in the long view, see Judith Jesch, *The Viking Diaspora* (London: Longman, 2015).
12. C. P. Lewis, 'Danish Landowners in Wessex in 1066', in *Danes in Wessex*, pp. 172–211. On the witness lists, see Mack, 'Changing Thegns', pp. 385–7.
13. *EHD*, p. 452; A. G. Kennedy, 'Cnut's Law Code of 1018', *Anglo-Saxon England*, 11 (1983), pp. 57–81.
14. 'Burial of Æthelred', pp. 142–3.
15. M. K. Lawson, 'Archbishop Wulfstan and the Homiletic Element in the Laws of Æthelred II and Cnut', in Rumble, p. 157.
16. *ASC* CDE 1017.
17. *Queen Emma*, pp. 174–8, addresses Emma's role in the 'Third Recension of the Second *Ordo*' in Corpus Christi College Cambridge MS 44. I am grateful to Liesbeth van Houts for discussion of this issue.
18. See 'Burial of Æthelred', particularly p. 143.
19. For comparison, see Geoffrey Koziol, *The Politics of Memory and Identity in Carolingian Royal Diplomas* (Turnhout: Brepols, 2012), particularly pp. 63–95. S 956, dating from 1019, indicates an earlier transaction, though this may have been a writ, a type of document that was increasingly common in the eleventh century; churches evidently issued their own leases, which perhaps made good some lacunae.
20. See S 951–6. Although not all these are the texts of 'genuine' charters, they may preserve names and titles of those (including Cnut) who attested actual charters.
21. Hearne, I, pp. 259–60.
22. Francesca Tinti, *Sustaining Belief: The Church of Worcester from c.870 to c.1100* (Aldershot: Ashgate, 2010), pp. 40–42, summarizes evidence of Wulfstan's continuing influence in Worcester after 1016.

23. For the 'Sermon of the Wolf', see Andreas Lemke, 'Fear-Mongering, Political Shrewdness or Setting the Stage for a Holy Society', *English Studies*, 95.7 (2014), pp. 758–76. Wulfstan's 'Institutes of Polity', rewritten for Cnut's reign, are translated by Andrew Rabin, in *The Political Writings of Archbishop Wulfstan of York* (Manchester: Manchester University Press, 2015), pp. 101–24.

24. Wormald, pp. 345–66.

25. *Empire of Cnut*, pp. 155–6, addresses the problematic evidence.

26. A valuable assessment of this is Clare Downham, *Viking Kings of Britain and Ireland* (Edinburgh: Dunedin Academic Press, 2007), whose consideration of English territory is at pp. 63–135.

27. *ASC* D 1017; 'Æthelings', pp. 181–3.

28. The Old Norse poem *Liðsmannaflokkr*, providing a dramatic rendition of the conquest of England, refers to a 'Lady' in a stone tower who may have been Emma in London. R. G. Poole, *Viking Poems on War and Peace* (Toronto: University of Toronto Press, 1991), pp. 86–90.

29. *II Cnut* 74, trans. *EHD*, p. 466.

30. *Encomium*, II.16, pp. 32–3, acknowledges the existence of sons from the first marriage.

31. Lawson, *Cnut*, p. 123, places her in England for much of Cnut's reign, partly on the basis of her Northampton appellation.

32. Ryan Lavelle, *Royal Estates in Anglo-Saxon England* (Oxford: Archaeopress, 2007), particularly pp. 99–101. On land within families, see Linda Tollerton, *Wills and Will-making in Anglo-Saxon England* (Woodbridge: Boydell Press, 2011), pp. 166–78.

33. The attempts that were made to delegitimize the second of Cnut and Ælfgifu's children, Harald, noted in *ASC* E 1035 and CD 1036, are relevant here, though the context in 1035 was different (see Chapter 6).

34. Asser, *Vita Ælfredi Regis*, ch. 75, in *Alfred the Great: Asser's Life of King Alfred and other Contemporary Sources*, trans. Simon Keynes and Michael Lapidge (Harmondsworth: Penguin, 1983), p. 90. This is discussed by Victoria Thompson, *Dying and Death in Later Anglo-Saxon England* (Woodbridge: Boydell Press, 2004), p. 9.

35. *Queen Emma*, p. 66, n. 3. On the 'unprecedented' number of new heirs, see Lavelle, *Aethelred II*, pp. 85–6.

36. A radically different suggestion for reference to 'the ætheling' in a will (S 1497) normally dated to between 990 and 1001, is that this was Harthacnut, dating it to about 1019. Kevin Kiernan, '*Beowulf* in the Age of Cnut: The Case for Late Square Old English Minuscule' (paper forthcoming).

3. FROM ENGLAND TO DENMARK

1. *ASC* CDE 1002; S 909.

2. See John Gillingham, '"The Most Precious Jewel in the English Crown": Levels of Danegeld and Heregeld in the Early Eleventh Century', *English Historical Review*, 104 (1989), pp. 373–84.

3. See Peter Sawyer, *The Wealth of Anglo-Saxon England* (Oxford: Oxford University Press, 2014), pp. 115–25.

4. *ASC* CDE 1018.

5. Harald is recorded (positively) as 'the King's Brother' in *Cnut Gospels* of Christ Church Canterbury: British Library Royal MS 1 D.IX, fol. 43v (online at http://www.bl.uk/manuscripts/FullDisplay.aspx?ref=Royal_MS_1_d_ix).

6. *Empire of Cnut*, p. 216; *Encomium*, II.2, pp. 18–19. Campbell's translation suggests that they *went* to 'the land of the Slavs', but the text itself could be read as sending for her; Thietmar, VII.39, pp. 334–5, relates her exile, hinting at conflict.

7. *The Life of King Edward who Rests at Westminster Attributed to a Monk of Saint-Bertin*, ed. Frank Barlow (Oxford: Oxford University Press, 2nd edn, 1992), ch. 1, pp. 10–11; for the context of these events and English earls in them, see Keynes, 'Cnut's Earls', pp. 82–5.

8. On urban development in Denmark under Cnut, see *Empire of Cnut*, pp. 159–75.

9. Dorothy Whitelock, M. Brett, Christopher Brooke and F. M. Powicke (eds), *Councils and Synods, with Other Documents Relating to the English Church: Volume I: A.D. 871–1204* (Oxford: Clarendon Press, 1981), Part 1, pp. 435–41, with commentary on p. 435; *EHD*, pp. 452–4.

10. Wormald, p. 348.

11. Thietmar, VIII.7, p. 366.

12. Stafford, 'Laws of Cnut', p. 187.

13. *ASC* C 1020.

14. Dorothy Bethurum, *The Homilies of Wulfstan* (Oxford: Oxford University Press, 1957), p. 35, with the sermon text at pp. 246–50; *ASC* CDF 1020. The Canterbury manuscript of the *ASC*, version F, records the detail of prayer for the souls of the men buried there.

15. *ASC* D 1021.

16. JW 1029, p. 510, has the record of Cnut's sister's marriage; a Slavic name is in the witness list of a 1026 Winchester charter, S 962; and the 'sister of Cnut, our king' is in the Winchester New Minster *Liber Vitae*, fol. 26v, in *Die Gedenküberlieferung der Angelsachsen*, ed. Jan Gerchow (Berlin: Walter de Gruyter, 1988), p. 325. This evidence is addressed by *Empire of Cnut*, pp. 211–18.

17. *ASC* D 1022 (C and E read 'Wiht'); *ASC* C 1023. Lund, 'Cnut's Danish Kingdom', pp. 36–7.

18. Keynes, 'Cnut's Earls', pp. 72–3.

19. 'Translatio Sancti Ælfegi Cantuariensis archiepiscopi et martiris', ed. Alexander R. Rumble and Rosemary Morris, in Rumble, pp. 283–315.

20. On Thorkell in Osbern's account, see Williams, 'Thorkell the Tall', p. 150.

21. Keynes, 'Cnut's Earls', p. 57; Williams, 'Thorkell the Tall', pp. 150–52.

22. *Empire of Cnut*, p. 219, citing Adam, II.54, p. 92.

23. Keynes, 'Cnut's Earls', pp. 62–4.

24. *ASC* E 1026. On the identification of Eilaf as the earl, see Keynes, 'Cnut's Earls', pp. 63–4.

25. The location of the battle is discussed in Peter Sawyer, 'Cnut's Scandinavian Empire', in Rumble, pp. 18–19.

26. *ASC* E 1026.

27. Keynes, 'Cnut's Earls', p. 60.

28. *Liber Vitae* of Thorney Abbey, fol. 10r, in *Die Gedenküberlieferung*, ed. Gerchow, p. 326. See Lawson, *Cnut*, pp. 123–4, and, for reservations, *Queen Emma*, p. 233.

29. Bolton, 'Ælfgifu of Northampton'.

30. *ASC* E 1035; *Encomium*, III.1, pp. 39–41.

31. Wipo, *Deeds of Conrad II*, ch. 35, in *Imperial Lives and Letters of the Eleventh Century*, trans. Theodor E. Mommsen and Karl F. Morrison (New York: Columbia University Press, 1962), p. 93.

32. *Empire of Cnut*, pp. 238–9.
33. For communication in 1036, see W. H. Stevenson, 'An Alleged Son of Harold Harefoot', *English Historical Review*, 28 (1913), pp. 112–17.

4. WIDER STILL, AND WIDER

1. *Tøgdrápa*, by Sighvat the Skald, in *EHD*, p. 338, stanza 6.
2. *Empire of Cnut*, pp. 244–5, citing the 'Oldest Saga of St Olaf' of *c.* 1200.
3. Wipo, *Deeds of Conrad II*, trans. Mommsen and Morrison, ch. 16, p. 79.
4. For Cnut and Conrad's relations, see Elaine Treharne, 'The Performance of Piety: Cnut, Rome, and England', in *England and Rome in the Early Middle Ages*, ed. Francesca Tinti (Turnhout: Brepols, 2014), pp. 344–6.
5. *EHD*, pp. 476–8 (quotation at p. 478). Keynes, 'Cnut's Earls', pp. 86–7, is circumspect about the extent of Earl Godwine's authority in this arrangement.
6. *EHD*, p. 476. The Latin text is in JW 1031, p. 512.
7. An important work here is L. M. Larson, *Canute the Great, 995 (circa)–1035, and the Rise of Danish Imperialism During the Viking Age* (New York: G. P. Putnam's Sons, 1912).
8. Sawyer, 'Cnut's Scandinavian Empire', pp. 18–20.
9. Ibid., pp. 19–20.
10. Birgit Sawyer, *The Viking-Age Rune-Stones* (Oxford: Oxford University Press, 2000), pp. 103–7.
11. Claus Krag, 'The Early Unification of Norway', in *The Cambridge History of Scandinavia*, vol. 1, ed. Helle, pp. 193–4.
12. Bill, 'Roskilde 6', p. 233.
13. See the 'Occasional Verses' by Sighvat the Skald, in *EHD*, pp. 339–40, stanza 16.
14. JW 1029, p. 510; Theodoric the Monk's account is cited by Whitelock in *ASC*, p. 101, n.
15. Sawyer, 'Cnut's Scandinavian Empire', p. 21.
16. *ASC* DE 1031.
17. *ASC* E 1031.
18. The date of 1031 is based on skaldic evidence and the Scottish rulers named in *ASC* E, by Benjamin T. Hudson, 'Cnut and the Scottish Kings', *English Historical Review*, 107 (1992), pp. 350–60.
19. *Encomium*, II.19, pp. 34–5. For even greater claims made of Cnut in the twelfth century, see Svein Aggeson, *Gestis Regum Danorum*, ch. 5, ed. G. Waitz, in *Monumenta Germaniae Historiae*, Scriptores 29 (Hanover: Hahn, 1892), p. 33.
20. *Empire of Cnut*, pp. 128–9.
21. Thomas Charles-Edwards, *Wales and the Britons, 350–1064* (Oxford: Oxford University Press, 2012), pp. 556–63.
22. Benjamin Hudson, 'Knútr and Viking Dublin', *Scandinavian Studies*, 66 (1994), pp. 319–35.
23. Simon Roffey and Ryan Lavelle, 'West Saxons and Danes: Negotiating Early Medieval Identities', in *Danes in Wessex*, p. 24.
24. S 949 is the most reliable of the charters purporting to be from Cnut. See 'Æthelings', p. 176, n. 18.
25. See Lesley Abrams, 'England, Normandy and Scandinavia', in *A Companion to the Anglo-Norman World*, ed. Christopher Harper-Bill and Elisabeth van Houts (Woodbridge: Boydell Press, 2003), pp. 46–50. The Scandinavian skald in Rouen

is detailed by David Bates, *Normandy Before 1066* (Harlow: Longman, 1982), p. 21, who discusses the 'final rupture' at pp. 23–4.

26. Adam, II.52, p. 92.

27. For a reading of the negotiation in the context of the aftermath of the abortive invasion of 1033, see Lawson, *Cnut*, pp. 106–7, and *Queen Emma*, pp. 234–5.

28. 'Æthelings', especially pp. 190–94, discussing the context of the record of the invasion reported by William of Jumièges, *The Gesta Normannorum Ducum of William of Jumièges, Orderic Vitalis and Robert of Torigni*, ed. and trans. E. M. C. van Houts, 2 vols (Oxford: Oxford University Press, 1992–5), I, pp. 76–9.

29. Sawyer, 'Cnut's Scandinavian Empire', p. 22.

5. INTO REALMS BEYOND

1. Geoffrey Koziol, 'Is Robert I in Hell? The Diploma for Saint-Denis and the Mind of a Rebel King (Jan. 25, 923)', *Early Medieval Europe*, 14.3 (2006), p. 263.

2. *EHD*, p. 896.

3. *EHD*, p. 476.

4. Treharne, 'The Performance of Piety', pp. 352–3.

5. H. R. Loyn, *The English Church 940–1154* (Harlow: Longman, 2000), pp. 49–50, provides a useful summary of Cnut's patronage. On eastern Danelaw churches, see *Empire of Cnut*, pp. 86–94.

6. Nicholas Brooks, 'History and Myth, Forgery and Truth', in *Anglo-Saxon Myths: State and Church* (London: Hambledon, 2000), p. 3.

7. S 745.

8. Wormald, pp. 346–8.

9. C. Karkov, *The Ruler Portraits of Anglo-Saxon England* (Woodbridge: Boydell Press, 2004), pp. 123–33.

10. Ibid., pp. 139–40.

11. Simon Keynes discusses the function of the *Liber Vitae*, in *The 'Liber Vitae' of the New Minster and Hyde Abbey, Winchester* (Copenhagen: Rosenkilde and Bagger, 1996), pp. 49–65.

12. Biddle and Kjølbye-Biddle, 'Danish Royal Burials in Winchester', pp. 224–6.

13. See generally Nicole Marafioti, *The King's Body: Burial and Succession in Late Anglo-Saxon England* (Toronto: Toronto University Press, 2014).

14. The link between the *Chronicle* and Cnut is suggested by Konshuh, '*Anraed* in their *Unraed*', pp. 158–9.

15. Lawson, *Cnut*, p. 130. The legal clause *I Cnut* 17.1, repeating Æthelred's earlier legislation (which may, itself, be a later addition to an Æthelredian manuscript), is translated in *The Laws of the Kings of England from Edmund to Henry I*, ed. A. J. Robertson (Cambridge: Cambridge University Press, 1925), pp. 168–9. Charters relating to the place of the body of Saint Edward at Shaftesbury are S 899 and 1503, discussed by Simon Keynes, 'King Alfred the Great and Shaftesbury Abbey', in *Studies in the Early History of Shaftesbury Abbey*, ed. Laurence Keen (Dorchester: Dorset County Council, 1999), pp. 55–6.

16. Lawson, *Cnut*, p. 130. For Edward's cult, see Ridyard, pp. 154–71.

17. Ridyard, pp. 151–3.

18. William of Malmesbury, *Gesta Pontificum Anglorum: The History of English Bishops*, vol. 1, ed. M. Winterbottom with R. M. Thomson (Oxford: Oxford University Press, 2007), pp. 298–301.

19. 'The *Translatio* of Edith', chs 12–13, trans. Michael Wright and Kathleen Lonhar, in *Writing the Wilton Women*, ed. Stephanie Hollis (Turnhout: Brepols, 2004), pp. 77–9.

20. Ridyard, pp. 153–4.

21. Martin Biddle, 'A Late Saxon Frieze Sculpture from Old Minster', *Antiquaries Journal*, 46 (1966), pp. 329–32. Biddle and Kjølbye-Biddle, 'Danish Royal Burials in Winchester', pp. 215–17.

22. J. J. G. Alexander, 'Sigmund or the King of the Garamantes?', in *Romanesque and Gothic: Essays for George Zarnecki*, ed. Neil Stratford, 2 vols (Woodbridge: Boydell Press, 1987), I, pp. 1–6.

23. Kevin S. Kiernan, *Beowulf and the Beowulf Manuscript* (Ann Arbor, Mich.: University of Michigan Press, 2nd edn, 1996); see debates addressed by Andy Orchard, *A Critical Companion to Beowulf* (Cambridge: D. S. Brewer, 2003), with Kiernan's thesis discussed at pp. 20–22.

24. Frank, 'King Cnut in the Verse of his Skalds', pp. 119–21.

25. Dominic Tweddle, Martin Biddle and Birthe Kjølbye-Biddle, *Corpus of Anglo-Saxon Stone Sculpture: Volume IV: South-East England* (Oxford: British Academy, 1995), pp. 327–8.

26. Adam, II.50, p. 91.

27. Jan Gerchow, 'Prayers for King Cnut: The Liturgical Commemoration of a Conqueror', in *England in the Eleventh Century*, ed. Carola Hicks (Stamford, Conn.: Paul Watkins, 1992), pp. 235–6.

28. A recent discussion of this phenomenon is Barbara Yorke, 'The Adaptation of the Anglo-Saxon Royal Courts to Christianity', in *The Cross Goes North*, ed. Martin Carver (Woodbridge: Boydell Press, 2003), pp. 244–5.

29. Michael Hare, 'Cnut and Lotharingia: Two Notes', *Anglo-Saxon England*, 29 (2000), pp. 261–78.

30. Adam, II.72, p. 107. Jean-Louis Kupper and Philippe George discuss tenth-century traditions in *Saint Lambert: De l'histoire à la légende* (Brussels: Luc Pire, 2006), p. 29.

31. *ASC* E 1022. See Nicholas Brooks, *The Early History of the Church of Canterbury* (Leicester: Leicester University Press, 1984), pp. 290–92.

32. Hill, 'An Urban Policy for Cnut?', p. 103, and Lawson, *Cnut*, pp. 131–2. However, cf. the wider issue of 'rapprochement' in 'Burial of Æthelred', p. 142.

33. Simeon of Durham, *Tract on the Origins and Progress of this, the Church of Durham*, ed. D. W. Rollason (Oxford: Oxford University Press, 2000), pp. 166–7. See also *Historia de Sancto Cuthberto*, ed. Ted Johnson South (Cambridge: D. S. Brewer, 2002), ch. 32, with the date of 1031 discussed at p. 114. The alternative date of 1018 is unlikely given Cnut's southern actions in that year (above, Chapter 2).

6. THE END OF DANISH ENGLAND

1. Roffey and Lavelle, 'West Saxons and Danes', pp. 23–5.

2. S 968.

3. Martin Gravel, *Distances, rencontres, communications: Réaliser l'empire sous Charlemagne et Louis le Pieux* (Turnhout: Brepols, 2012), pp. 27–94.

4. Matthew Townend, 'Contextualizing the *Knútsdrápur*: Skaldic Praise-Poetry at the Court of Cnut', *Anglo-Saxon England*, 30 (2001), pp. 145–79.

5. *ASC* C 1030.

6. *ASC* E 1035.

7. William of Jumièges, I, pp. 78–9.

8. Frank, 'King Cnut in the Verse of his Skalds', p. 120.

9. Lawson, *Cnut*, p. 193.

10. *King Harald's Saga*, trans. Magnus Magnusson and Hermann Pálsson (Harmondsworth: Penguin, 1966), p. 158.

Further Reading

This book was completed as a new biography of Cnut by Timothy Bolton came off the press: *Cnut the Great* (New Haven, Conn., and London: Yale University Press, 2017). Given the depth of research in the same author's broader study, *The Empire of Cnut the Great* (Leiden and Boston: Brill, 2009), the biography looks set to be the standard work on the ruler for some years to come. The earliest full study of Cnut in English, L. M. Larson, *Canute the Great, 995 (circa)–1035, and the Rise of Danish Imperialism during the Viking Age* (New York and London: G. P. Putnam's Sons, 1912), though of its time in proudly bearing the author's view of Scandinavian exceptionalism, remains an impressive piece of scholarship. Building on the work of many of the contemporary Scandinavian historians, Larson is noteworthy in his early engagement with the problems of reliability of sources from more than a century after the events of Cnut's day, even if he ultimately relies on them to build up a dramatic story. M. K. Lawson, *Cnut: England's Viking King* (Stroud: Tempus, 2004), first printed as *Cnut: The Danes in England in the Eleventh Century* (London: Longman, 1993), takes a less favourable view of Cnut's 'imperial' achievements than Larson or Bolton, focusing on the institutions that determined the shape of Cnut's English kingdom and its limits, though it remains an excellent and comprehensive study. An essay collection, *The Reign of Cnut*, edited by Alexander Rumble (London: Leicester University Press, 1994), is a useful snapshot of aspects of the reign.

The broader setting of political development, focusing on the structures of politics as well as the individual rulers, is established by Pauline Stafford, *Unification and Conquest: A Political and Social*

History of England in the Tenth and Eleventh Centuries (London: Hodder & Stoughton, 1989), while the same author teases out some of the strands of queenly power in *Queen Emma and Queen Edith: Queenship and Women's Power in Eleventh-Century England* (Oxford: Blackwell, 1997). The most recent biography addressing the reign of Cnut's predecessor Æthelred – with considerations of the political kingdoms leading to Cnut's takeover – is Levi Roach, *Æthelred the Unready* (New Haven, Conn., and London: Yale University Press, 2016). Edmund Ironside awaits his biographer, though Charles Insley, 'Politics, Conflict and Kinship in Early Eleventh-Century Mercia', *Midland History*, 25 (2000), pp. 28–42, provides a valuable indication of how and why he managed to stir the factional pot in this period.

Of the other remarkable individuals in Cnut's reign, the first chapters of Frank Barlow, *The Godwins: The Rise and Fall of a Noble Dynasty* (Harlow: Longman, 2002), are a recent attempt to flesh out the story of Godwine's early career, while Robin Fleming, *Kings and Lords in Conquest England* (Cambridge: Cambridge University Press, 1993), provides some context of the landed wealth of Godwine and other earls under Cnut. An alternative reading, though focused less on the period before Edward the Confessor than during his reign, is Stephen Baxter, *The Earls of Mercia: Lordship and Power in Late Anglo-Saxon England* (Oxford: Oxford University Press, 2007), while W. E. Kapelle, *The Norman Conquest of the North: The Region and its Transformation, 1000–1135* (Chapel Hill, NC: University of North Carolina Press, 1979), provides considerable context to the Cnut-era independence of northern magnates such as Earl Uhtred. On the figure who bridged the gap between the reigns of Æthelred and Cnut, the collection edited by Matthew Townend, *Wulfstan, Archbishop of York* (Turnhout: Brepols, 2004), offers valuable perspectives, while Patrick Wormald, *The Making of English Law: King Alfred to the Twelfth Century: Volume I: Legislation and its Limits* (Oxford: Blackwell, 1999), has even more to say about Wulfstan's legal legacy as well as other texts from Cnut's reign. Other bishops are discussed in Mary Frances Giandrea, *Episcopal Culture in Late Anglo-Saxon England* (Woodbridge: Boydell Press, 2007).

Despite its title, Ryan Lavelle, *Alfred's Wars: Sources and Interpretations of Anglo-Saxon Warfare in the Viking Age* (Woodbridge: Boydell Press, 2010), takes discussion through to the Viking wars of Cnut and the military developments of the period, an issue first addressed in some detail by Nicholas Hooper in his contribution to Rumble's 1994 volume cited above. A rich sense of the material culture of the Vikings in this period, including, of course, the 'Roskilde 6' longship, is provided by a volume edited by Gareth Williams, Peter Pentz and Matthias Wemhoff, *Vikings: Life and Legend* (London: British Museum Press, 2014). Another collection, *Danes in Wessex: The Scandinavian Impact on Southern England, c.800–c.1100*, edited by Ryan Lavelle and Simon Roffey (Oxford: Oxbow, 2016), includes, among perspectives on Scandinavian settlers provided by Ann Williams and Chris Lewis, an English-language version of the article by Martin Biddle and Birthe Kjølbye-Biddle setting out the evidence for the bones of Cnut in his final resting place: a dynastic mausoleum in Winchester Cathedral.

Picture Credits

1. Cnut with Emma, frontispiece of *Liber Vitae* ('Book of Life', 1031). British Library, London, BL Stowe 944, fol. 6r (© British Library Board. All Rights Reserved/Bridgeman Images)

2. Possible representation of Cnut, verso of the frontispiece of *Liber Vitae*, 1031. British Library, London, BL Stowe 944, fol. 6v (© British Library Board. All Rights Reserved/Bridgeman Images)

3. Coin depicting Cnut as a warrior, *c.* 1024–30 (Edgar L. Owen, Ltd)

4. Early-modern bone chest said to contain the bones of Cnut, Winchester Cathedral (© Richard Purkiss)

5. Cnut in combat with King Edmund Ironside at the Battle of Assandun, from Matthew Paris, *Chronica Majora*, thirteenth century. Corpus Christi College, Cambridge MS 26, fol. 80v (The Master and Fellows of Corpus Christi College, Cambridge)

6. Queen Emma, frontispiece of *Encomium Emmae Reginae*, eleventh century. British Library, London, Add 33241 fol. 1v (© British Library Board. All Rights Reserved/Bridgeman Images)

7. Pharoah with his witan, from the *Old English Hexateuch*, 1025–50. British Library, London, Cotton Claudius B IV fol. 59 (© British Library Board. All Rights Reserved/Bridgeman Images)

8. Deerhurst Church, Gloucestershire (Alamy)

9. Runestone erected at Jelling, Jutland, Denmark, by Harald 'Bluetooth', probably in the 960s (Alamy)

10. 'Roskilde 6', partially reconstructed for the exhibition 'Vikings: Life and Legend', British Museum, London, 2014 (© Paul Raftery)

11. Charter of Cnut granting the estate at Drayton to the community of the New Minster, Winchester, 1019. Winchester College Archives (The Warden and Scholars of Winchester College)

12. Part of a narrative frieze, stone, probably 1016–35, from the site of the Old Minster, Winchester (John Crook/Winchester Excavations Committee)

13. Olaf of Norway, from a thirteenth-century altarpiece at Trondheim Cathedral, Norway (Alamy)

14. Modern representation of 'Knud den Store' (Cnut the Great), National Museum, Denmark (© Foto Lennart Larsen, Nationalmuseet)

15. 'King Canute Defies the Waves', 1964, illustration by James E. McConnell for Look and Learn (© Look and Learn/Bridgeman Images)

Acknowledgements

Writing this book has benefited from discussion with friends, family members and colleagues: Richard Abels, Karl Alvestad, David Bates, Ellora Bennett, Timothy Bolton, Carolin Esser-Miles, Liesbeth van Houts, Charles Insley, Kevin Kiernan, Courtnay Konshuh, Eric Lacey, Don and Vee Lavelle, Janine Lavelle, David McDermott, Simon Roffey, Katherine Weikert, Gareth Williams and Barbara Yorke, as well as two cohorts of students from my 'Second Viking Age' special study at Winchester. I'm particularly grateful to Barbara and Karl for reading through drafts of this book for its academic content, as well as to my harshest (but, on balance, fairest) critics, my mother, Vee Lavelle, and my editors at Penguin, Simon Winder and Kate Parker, who helped me to shape the final text.

I am also grateful to Professor Roberta Frank for granting me permission to quote from her translation of the *Knútsdrápa* of Hallvarðr Háreksblesi in Chapter 6, and to Oxford University Press for allowing me to quote from Diana Greenway's translation of Henry of Huntingdon in Chapter 1.

I wish to dedicate this book to Benjamin, whose moral universe and occasional interest in Vikings have begun to develop as this book took shape. In response to his question 'Was *that man* a goodie or a baddie?', I have only been able to offer that Cnut was a bit of both and a lot between. I hope that as Benjamin grows up he is granted an appreciation of humanity that allows him to understand what I meant.

Index

Aachen 83
Adam of Bremen 65,
  79–80
Ælfgifu of Northampton
  10–11, 13, 15, 35, 37, 38,
  52–3, 54, 66, 88
Ælfheah, Archbishop of
  Canterbury, Saint 49–50,
  73, 81
Ælfheah of Devonshire 28
Ælfthryth, Queen 75
Æthelmær 22–3, 28
Æthelnoth, Archbishop of
  Canterbury 81
Æthelred 'the Unready', King of
  the English 7–8, 10, 11–15,
  16–17, 18–19, 20, 27, 28, 29,
  31, 32, 33, 35, 36, 38, 39, 40,
  44, 48, 73, 74–5
Æthelstan, King of the
  English 68
Æthelweard (nobleman
  executed in 1017) 28, 29
Æthelweard (ealdorman) 46
Æthelwine 6–7
Æthelwulf, King of the West
  Saxons 45, 68
Alfred the Great, King of the
  West Saxons 16, 24, 35, 39,
  68, 73
Anglo-Saxon Chronicle x–xi,
  5–6, 10, 12, 13, 16, 17–18,
  21, 22, 23, 24, 25, 26, 27,
  31–2, 36, 39, 40–1, 43, 45,

46, 47–8, 51, 59, 60, 62, 73,
  83, 84
Anund Jacob, King of Sweden
  55, 57, 58, 59
Assandun, Battle of 21, 23,
  46–7

Baltic, the 5, 42, 57, 84
Bath 22
Beorhtric 28
Beowulf 77–8
Bolesław Chobry, King of
  Poland 47
Bosham 4

Caithness 62
Canterbury 31, 39, 49, 68, 81
Charlemagne, Holy Roman
  Emperor 60, 78, 83
Chartres, Fulbert, Bishop of 67
Cirencester 45
Cnut, King of the English,
  Denmark and Norway:
  attempt to stop the tide 3–4;
  in popular history 3–5; use of
  violence 5–7, 9, 12–13, 27–9,
  30, 52, 69, 82, 87–8; mother
  8, 54, 80; family background
  8–10; Christian heritage 9;
  marriage to Ælfgifu 10–11,
  13, 15, 52–3, 54; marriage to
  Emma 10, 11, 32, 35–9, 52,
  53–4, 56, 64, 71–2; death of
  Swein Forkbeard 11–12; and

the second reign of Æthelred 12–13; in Denmark 13–15; return to England 14, 15, 15–16; conquest of England 16–24; coinage 20–1; consolidation of power 25–39; opposition to 29–30; coronation 31–2; first charters 32–3; and Wulfstan 33–4; law codes 34; legitimation 35, 44–5, 71, 74; bigamy 37; children 38–9, 52–4, 56; Danish kingdom 40–5, 49, 50–2, 54, 56–7; domination of the English kingdom 45–7; break with Thorkell 47–8; reconciliation with Thorkell 48–50; Christianity 50, 67–82; death of Thorkell 50–1; Holy River campaign 51–2, 55, 57–8, 59, 65, 87; visit to Rome 55–7, 59, 62, 68; Swedish claims 57–8, 62, 63; Norwegian claims 58–61, 63, 84; empire 62, 63, 86; Scottish surrender to 62–3, 82; Welsh overlordship 63; as pagan 67, 70, 77–80; ecclesiastical patronage 68–9, 72, 75–6; depictions of 69–72; family policy 74–6; baptismal name 80; death of 82, 83, 84–5; final years 83–5; legacy 85–8; assessment of 87–8

Cnut, King of York 35
Cnut IV, King of Denmark, Saint 82
Conrad, Holy Roman Emperor 55–6, 70
Cosham 16–17
Cuthbert, Saint 81

Deerhurst 22
Denmark 5, 8, 9, 13–15, 18, 26, 34, 40–5, 46, 48–9, 50–2, 52, 53, 54, 56, 74, 79–80, 84, 88
Dorset 16
Dublin 63–4
Durham 9–10, 18, 68, 81–2

Eadred, King of the English 29
Eadric 'Streona' ('Acquisitor') 21, 26, 27, 27–8, 29
Eadwig, 'King of the Ceorls' 45
Eadwig (son of Æthelred) 24, 27, 29
East Anglia 26, 35, 68
Edgar, King of the English 24, 29, 39, 42, 44, 68, 70, 73, 75
Edith, Saint 75–6
Edmund, King of the East Angles, Saint 11
Edmund 'Ironside', King of the English 15, 17, 19–25, 28, 35, 38, 72–4, 83, 88
Edward the Confessor, King of the English 31, 64, 65–6, 68, 86–7
Edward 'the Martyr', King of the English 73, 74–5, 82
Eilaf 51, 63
Emma, Queen 10, 11, 32, 35–9, 52, 53–4, 56, 64, 71–2, 75, 76
Encomium Emma Reginae x–xi, 8, 14, 23, 36, 57, 63
England 4, 5–8, 9–10, 11–15, 16–23, 26–39, 40–1, 45–7, 48–50, 52, 53–4, 56–7, 59, 85–8
English Channel 4, 16
Erik 'Bloodaxe', King of York 35
Erik, Jarl of Lade 26, 59
Essex 21

Estrith 50, 65
Exeter 80

Flanders 25
France 86

Gainsborough 10, 11, 13
Germany 78
Ghent 25
Gillingham 20
Glastonbury 72, 73, 83
Godwine, Earl of Wessex 48, 49
Goscelin of Saint-Bertin 75-6
Gruffudd ap Llywellyn, King of
  Gwynnedd 63
Gunnhild (daughter of Cnut)
  53, 54, 56, 61
Gunnhild (niece of Cnut) 60, 61
Guthrum, King of the East
  Anglian Vikings 35
Gytha 8

Håkon, Jarl of Lade 60-1, 88
Harald, King of Denmark 8,
  15, 34, 41-2, 57
Harald 'Bluetooth', King of
  Denmark 8, 9, 42, 58, 79
Harald 'Hardrada', King of
  Norway 86
Harald 'Harefoot' 38, 50-1,
  52-3, 84, (as King of the
  English) 85-6
Harold Godwinesson, King of
  the English 86
Harthacnut 29, 39, 50, 53, 54,
  74, (as King of Denmark and
  of the English) 86
Henry I, King of England 31
Henry of Huntingdon 3-4, 5,
  22-3
'Holy River', Battle of 51-2, 55,
  57-8, 59, 65, 87

Isle of Wight 10, 47-8

Jelling 8
John of Worcester 20, 23-4,
  25, 60

Kent 16
Kingston-upon-Thames 31
Koziol, Geoffrey 67

Lambert, Bishop of Maastricht-
  Liège, Saint 80
Leofwine 28
Lincolnshire 35
Lindsey 13
London 14, 19-20, 25, 27-8,
  31, 32, 36, 40, 49, 81, 84
Lyfing, Archbishop of
  Canterbury 31

Mælbæth, Scottish ruler 62
Magnus, King of Norway 66
Malcolm, King of the Scots 62
Mary Magdalene 71
Mercia 22, 24, 26
Mont-Saint-Michel 65
Morcar 15

Normandy 10, 35-6, 37, 64-6,
  74, 86, 87
North Sea 5, 16, 42, 44, 45, 54,
  86, 87
Northumbria 17-18, 26,
  35, 83
Norway 5, 8, 26, 51, 52, 54,
  58-61, 63, 66, 74, 83, 84, 88
Norwegian Sea 42

Odda of Deerhurst 22, 28-9
Olaf Haraldsson, King of
  Norway (later Saint) 51, 55,
  58-9, 60, 61, 66, 79, 84

Olaf Sihtricsson, Viking king of Dublin and York 35
Olaf Tryggvasson, King of Norway 79
Olney-by-Deerhurst 22
Orkney 61, 62
Ottar the Black 9
Oxford 40, 44, 73

Pentland Firth 60
Poland 47, 80
Portsmouth 17

Ralph de Diceto, Dean of St Paul's 31
Richard II, Duke of Normandy 35, 64, 65
Robert I, King of the Franks 67
Robert the Magnificent, Duke of Normandy 64-5
Rome 55-7, 59, 62, 68, 72, 83
Roskilde 51-2

Sandwich 5-7, 12-13, 14, 15
'Santslaue' 47, 60
Scotland 62-3, 82, 83
Severn, River 22
Shaftesbury 82, 83, 84-5
Shaftesbury Abbey 74
Shakespeare, William 62
Shetland 62
Sigeferth 15
Sighvat 55
Sigmund (character in Völsunga Saga) 76-7
Sjælland 55
Skåne 47, 50, 51, 55, 57
Somerset 16
Southampton 4, 20
Stephen, King of England 31
Stiklestad 61, 66, 84

Sweden 5, 51, 57-8, 62, 63
Swein 38, 50-1, 52-3, 61, 66, 74, 88
Swein 'Forkbeard', King of Denmark and of the English 6, 7-8, 9-10, 11-13, 14, 18, 22, 35, 41, 54, 57, 70, 79-80

Thietmar of Merseburg 15, 44
Thorkell Skallason 88
Thorkell 'the Tall' 8, 14-15, 16, 19, 26, 43, 46-7, 46-51, 81
Thorney Abbey 52
Trøndelag, the 61

Uhtred, Earl 17-8, 82
Ulf Thorgilsson 50, 51-2, 65
Uppland 51, 57-8

Wales 63
Wessex 16-17, 20-1, 22, 26, 27, 30, 68, 85
Westminster 4
'Wihtland' 47-8, 53
William I, King of England 85-6
William of Jumièges 65, 84-5
Wilton Abbey 75-6
Wiltshire 16
Winchester 16, 31, 40, 72, 76-7, 79, 81, 82, 83
Worcestershire 7
Wulfnoth 48
Wulfstan, Archbishop of York 12, 18, 31-2, 33-4, 44-5, 46-7, 70, 75, 78, 81
'Wyrtgeorn', King of the Wends 60

York 17, 18, 44-5, 68, 83

Penguin Monarchs

THE HOUSES OF WESSEX AND DENMARK

Athelstan	Tom Holland
Aethelred the Unready	Richard Abels
Cnut	Ryan Lavelle

THE HOUSES OF NORMANDY, BLOIS AND ANJOU

William I	Marc Morris
William II	John Gillingham
Henry I	Edmund King
Stephen	Carl Watkins
Henry II	Richard Barber
Richard I	Thomas Asbridge
John	Nicholas Vincent

THE HOUSE OF PLANTAGENET

Henry III	Stephen Church
Edward I	Andy King
Edward II	Christopher Given-Wilson
Edward III	Jonathan Sumption
Richard II	Laura Ashe

THE HOUSES OF LANCASTER AND YORK

Henry IV	Catherine Nall
Henry V	Anne Curry
Henry VI	James Ross
Edward IV	A. J. Pollard
Edward V	Thomas Penn
Richard III	Rosemary Horrox

THE HOUSE OF TUDOR

Henry VII	Sean Cunningham
Henry VIII	John Guy
Edward VI	Stephen Alford
Mary I	John Edwards
Elizabeth I	Helen Castor

THE HOUSE OF STUART

James I	Thomas Cogswell
Charles I	Mark Kishlansky
[Cromwell	David Horspool]
Charles II	Clare Jackson
James II	David Womersley
William III & Mary II	Jonathan Keates
Anne	Richard Hewlings

THE HOUSE OF HANOVER

George I	Tim Blanning
George II	Norman Davies
George III	Amanda Foreman
George IV	Stella Tillyard
William IV	Roger Knight
Victoria	Jane Ridley

THE HOUSES OF SAXE-COBURG & GOTHA AND WINDSOR

Edward VII	Richard Davenport-Hines
George V	David Cannadine
Edward VIII	Piers Brendon
George VI	Philip Ziegler
Elizabeth II	Douglas Hurd

ALLEN LANE
an imprint of
PENGUIN BOOKS

Also Published

Clare Jackson, *Devil-Land: England Under Siege, 1588-1688*

Steven Pinker, *Rationality: Why It Is, Why It Seems Scarce, Why It Matters*

Volker Ullrich, *Eight Days in May: How Germany's War Ended*

Adam Tooze, *Shutdown: How Covide Shook the World's Economy*

Tristram Hunt, *The Radical Potter: Josiah Wedgwood and the Transformation of Britain*

Paul Davies, *What's Eating the Universe: And Other Cosmic Questions*

Shon Faye, *The Transgender Issue: An Argument for Justice*

Dennis Duncan, *Index, A History of the*

Richard Overy, *Blood and Ruins: The Great Imperial War, 1931-1945*

Paul Mason, *How to Stop Fascism: History, Ideology, Resistance*

Cass R. Sunstein and Richard H. Thaler, *Nudge: Improving Decisions About Health, Wealth and Happiness*

Lisa Miller, *The Awakened Brain: The Psychology of Spirituality and Our Search for Meaning*

Michael Pye, *Antwerp: The Glory Years*

Christopher Clark, *Prisoners of Time: Prussians, Germans and Other Humans*

Rupa Marya and Raj Patel, *Inflamed: Deep Medicine and the Anatomy of Injustice*

Richard Zenith, *Pessoa: An Experimental Life*

Michael Pollan, *This Is Your Mind On Plants: Opium—Caffeine—Mescaline*

Amartya Sen, *Home in the World: A Memoir*

Jan-Werner Müller, *Democracy Rules*

Robin DiAngelo, *Nice Racism: How Progressive White People Perpetuate Racial Harm*

Rosemary Hill, *Time's Witness: History in the Age of Romanticism*

Lawrence Wright, *The Plague Year: America in the Time of Covid*

Adrian Wooldridge, *The Aristocracy of Talent: How Meritocracy Made the Modern World*

Julian Hoppit, *The Dreadful Monster and its Poor Relations: Taxing, Spending and the United Kingdom, 1707-2021*

Jordan Ellenberg, *Shape: The Hidden Geometry of Absolutely Everything*

Duncan Campbell-Smith, *Crossing Continents: A History of Standard Chartered Bank*

Jemma Wadham, *Ice Rivers*

Niall Ferguson, *Doom: The Politics of Catastrophe*

Michael Lewis, *The Premonition: A Pandemic Story*

Chiara Marletto, *The Science of Can and Can't: A Physicist's Journey Through the Land of Counterfactuals*

Suzanne Simard, *Finding the Mother Tree: Uncovering the Wisdom and Intelligence of the Forest*

Giles Fraser, *Chosen: Lost and Found between Christianity and Judaism*

Malcolm Gladwell, *The Bomber Mafia: A Story Set in War*

Kate Darling, *The New Breed: How to Think About Robots*

Serhii Plokhy, *Nuclear Folly: A New History of the Cuban Missile Crisis*

Sean McMeekin, *Stalin's War*

Michio Kaku, *The God Equation: The Quest for a Theory of Everything*

Michael Barber, *Accomplishment: How to Achieve Ambitious and Challenging Things*

Charles Townshend, *The Partition: Ireland Divided, 1885-1925*

Hanif Abdurraqib, *A Little Devil in America: In Priase of Black Performance*

Carlo Rovelli, *Helgoland*

Herman Pontzer, *Burn: The Misunderstood Science of Metabolism*

Jordan B. Peterson, *Beyond Order: 12 More Rules for Life*

Bill Gates, *How to Avoid a Climate Disaster: The Solutions We Have and the Breakthroughs We Need*

Kehinde Andrews, *The New Age of Empire: How Racism and Colonialism Still Rule the World*

Veronica O'Keane, *The Rag and Bone Shop: How We Make Memories and Memories Make Us*

Robert Tombs, *This Sovereign Isle: Britain In and Out of Europe*

Mariana Mazzucato, *Mission Economy: A Moonshot Guide to Changing Capitalism*

Frank Wilczek, *Fundamentals: Ten Keys to Reality*

Milo Beckman, *Math Without Numbers*

John Sellars, *The Fourfold Remedy: Epicurus and the Art of Happiness*

T. G. Otte, *Statesman of Europe: A Life of Sir Edward Grey*

Alex Kerr, *Finding the Heart Sutra: Guided by a Magician, an Art Collector and Buddhist Sages from Tibet to Japan*

Edwin Gale, *The Species That Changed Itself: How Prosperity Reshaped Humanity*

Simon Baron-Cohen, *The Pattern Seekers: A New Theory of Human Invention*

Christopher Harding, *The Japanese: A History of Twenty Lives*

Carlo Rovelli, *There Are Places in the World Where Rules Are Less Important Than Kindness*

Ritchie Robertson, *The Enlightenment: The Pursuit of Happiness 1680-1790*

Ivan Krastev, *Is It Tomorrow Yet?: Paradoxes of the Pandemic*

Tim Harper, *Underground Asia: Global Revolutionaries and the Assault on Empire*

John Gray, *Feline Philosophy: Cats and the Meaning of Life*

Priya Satia, *Time's Monster: History, Conscience and Britain's Empire*

Fareed Zakaria, *Ten Lessons for a Post-Pandemic World*

David Sumpter, *The Ten Equations that Rule the World: And How You Can Use Them Too*

Richard J. Evans, *The Hitler Conspiracies: The Third Reich and the Paranoid Imagination*

Fernando Cervantes, *Conquistadores*

John Darwin, *Unlocking the World: Port Cities and Globalization in the Age of Steam, 1830-1930*

Michael Strevens, *The Knowledge Machine: How an Unreasonable Idea Created Modern Science*

Owen Jones, *This Land: The Story of a Movement*

Seb Falk, *The Light Ages: A Medieval Journey of Discovery*

Daniel Yergin, *The New Map: Energy, Climate, and the Clash of Nations*

Michael J. Sandel, *The Tyranny of Merit: What's Become of the Common Good?*

Joseph Henrich, *The Weirdest People in the World: How the West Became Psychologically Peculiar and Particularly Prosperous*

Leonard Mlodinow, *Stephen Hawking: A Memoir of Friendship and Physics*

David Goodhart, *Head Hand Heart: The Struggle for Dignity and Status in the 21st Century*

Claudia Rankine, *Just Us: An American Conversation*

James Rebanks, *English Pastoral: An Inheritance*

Robin Lane Fox, *The Invention of Medicine: From Homer to Hippocrates*

Daniel Lieberman, *Exercised: The Science of Physical Activity, Rest and Health*

Sudhir Hazareesingh, *Black Spartacus: The Epic Life of Touissaint Louverture*

Judith Herrin, *Ravenna: Capital of Empire, Crucible of Europe*

Samantha Cristoforetti, *Diary of an Apprentice Astronaut*

Neil Price, *The Children of Ash and Elm: A History of the Vikings*

George Dyson, *Analogia: The Entangled Destinies of Nature, Human Beings and Machines*

Wolfram Eilenberger, *Time of the Magicians: The Invention of Modern Thought, 1919-1929*

Kate Manne, *Entitled: How Male Privilege Hurts Women*

Christopher de Hamel, *The Book in the Cathedral: The Last Relic of Thomas Becket*

Isabel Wilkerson, *Caste: The International Bestseller*

Bradley Garrett, *Bunker: Building for the End Times*

Katie Mack, *The End of Everything: (Astrophysically Speaking)*

Jonathan C. Slaght, *Owls of the Eastern Ice: The Quest to Find and Save the World's Largest Owl*

Carl T. Bergstrom and Jevin D. West, *Calling Bullshit: The Art of Scepticism in a Data-Driven World*

Paul Collier and John Kay, *Greed Is Dead: Politics After Individualism*

Anne Applebaum, *Twilight of Democracy: The Failure of Politics and the Parting of Friends*

Sarah Stewart Johnson, *The Sirens of Mars: Searching for Life on Another World*

Martyn Rady, *The Habsburgs: The Rise and Fall of a World Power*

John Gooch, *Mussolini's War: Fascist Italy from Triumph to Collapse, 1935-1943*

Roger Scruton, *Wagner's Parsifal: The Music of Redemption*

Roberto Calasso, *The Celestial Hunter*

Benjamin R. Teitelbaum, *War for Eternity: The Return of Traditionalism and the Rise of the Populist Right*

Laurence C. Smith, *Rivers of Power: How a Natural Force Raised Kingdoms, Destroyed Civilizations, and Shapes Our World*

Sharon Moalem, *The Better Half: On the Genetic Superiority of Women*

Augustine Sedgwick, *Coffeeland: A History*

Daniel Todman, *Britain's War: A New World, 1942-1947*

Anatol Lieven, *Climate Change and the Nation State: The Realist Case*

Blake Gopnik, *Warhol: A Life as Art*

Malena and Beata Ernman, Svante and Greta Thunberg, *Our House is on Fire: Scenes of a Family and a Planet in Crisis*

Paolo Zellini, *The Mathematics of the Gods and the Algorithms of Men: A Cultural History*

Bari Weiss, *How to Fight Anti-Semitism*

Lucy Jones, *Losing Eden: Why Our Minds Need the Wild*

Brian Greene, *Until the End of Time: Mind, Matter, and Our Search for Meaning in an Evolving Universe*

Anastasia Nesvetailova and Ronen Palan, *Sabotage: The Business of Finance*

Albert Costa, *The Bilingual Brain: And What It Tells Us about the Science of Language*

Stanislas Dehaene, *How We Learn: The New Science of Education and the Brain*

Daniel Susskind, *A World Without Work: Technology, Automation and How We Should Respond*

John Tierney and Roy F. Baumeister, *The Power of Bad: And How to Overcome It*

Greta Thunberg, *No One Is Too Small to Make a Difference: Illustrated Edition*

Glenn Simpson and Peter Fritsch, *Crime in Progress: The Secret History of the Trump-Russia Investigation*

Abhijit V. Banerjee and Esther Duflo, *Good Economics for Hard Times: Better Answers to Our Biggest Problems*

Gaia Vince, *Transcendence: How Humans Evolved through Fire, Language, Beauty and Time*

Roderick Floud, *An Economic History of the English Garden*

Rana Foroohar, *Don't Be Evil: The Case Against Big Tech*

Ivan Krastev and Stephen Holmes, *The Light that Failed: A Reckoning*

Andrew Roberts, *Leadership in War: Lessons from Those Who Made History*

Alexander Watson, *The Fortress: The Great Siege of Przemysl*

Stuart Russell, *Human Compatible: AI and the Problem of Control*

Serhii Plokhy, *Forgotten Bastards of the Eastern Front: An Untold Story of World War II*

Dominic Sandbrook, *Who Dares Wins: Britain, 1979-1982*

Charles Moore, *Margaret Thatcher: The Authorized Biography, Volume Three: Herself Alone*

Thomas Penn, *The Brothers York: An English Tragedy*

David Abulafia, *The Boundless Sea: A Human History of the Oceans*

Anthony Aguirre, *Cosmological Koans: A Journey to the Heart of Physics*

Orlando Figes, *The Europeans: Three Lives and the Making of a Cosmopolitan Culture*

Naomi Klein, *On Fire: The Burning Case for a Green New Deal*

Anne Boyer, *The Undying: A Meditation on Modern Illness*

Benjamin Moser, *Sontag: Her Life*

Daniel Markovits, *The Meritocracy Trap*

Malcolm Gladwell, *Talking to Strangers: What We Should Know about the People We Don't Know*

Peter Hennessy, *Winds of Change: Britain in the Early Sixties*

John Sellars, *Lessons in Stoicism: What Ancient Philosophers Teach Us about How to Live*

Brendan Simms, *Hitler: Only the World Was Enough*

Hassan Damluji, *The Responsible Globalist: What Citizens of the World Can Learn from Nationalism*

Peter Gatrell, *The Unsettling of Europe: The Great Migration, 1945 to the Present*

Justin Marozzi, *Islamic Empires: Fifteen Cities that Define a Civilization*

Bruce Hood, *Possessed: Why We Want More Than We Need*

Susan Neiman, *Learning from the Germans: Confronting Race and the Memory of Evil*

Donald D. Hoffman, *The Case Against Reality: How Evolution Hid the Truth from Our Eyes*

Frank Close, *Trinity: The Treachery and Pursuit of the Most Dangerous Spy in History*

Richard M. Eaton, *India in the Persianate Age: 1000-1765*

Janet L. Nelson, *King and Emperor: A New Life of Charlemagne*

Philip Mansel, *King of the World: The Life of Louis XIV*

Donald Sassoon, *The Anxious Triumph: A Global History of Capitalism, 1860-1914*

Elliot Ackerman, *Places and Names: On War, Revolution and Returning*

Jonathan Aldred, *Licence to be Bad: How Economics Corrupted Us*

Johny Pitts, *Afropean: Notes from Black Europe*

Walt Odets, *Out of the Shadows: Reimagining Gay Men's Lives*

James Lovelock, *Novacene: The Coming Age of Hyperintelligence*

Mark B. Smith, *The Russia Anxiety: And How History Can Resolve It*

Stella Tillyard, *George IV: King in Waiting*

Jonathan Rée, *Witcraft: The Invention of Philosophy in English*

Jared Diamond, *Upheaval: How Nations Cope with Crisis and Change*

Emma Dabiri, *Don't Touch My Hair*

Srecko Horvat, *Poetry from the Future: Why a Global Liberation Movement Is Our Civilisation's Last Chance*

Paul Mason, *Clear Bright Future: A Radical Defence of the Human Being*

Remo H. Largo, *The Right Life: Human Individuality and its role in our development, health and happiness*

Joseph Stiglitz, *People, Power and Profits: Progressive Capitalism for an Age of Discontent*

David Brooks, *The Second Mountain*

Roberto Calasso, *The Unnamable Present*

Lee Smolin, *Einstein's Unfinished Revolution: The Search for What Lies Beyond the Quantum*

Clare Carlisle, *Philosopher of the Heart: The Restless Life of Søren Kierkegaard*

Nicci Gerrard, *What Dementia Teaches Us About Love*

Edward O. Wilson, *Genesis: On the Deep Origin of Societies*

John Barton, *A History of the Bible: The Book and its Faiths*

Carolyn Forché, *What You Have Heard is True: A Memoir of Witness and Resistance*

Elizabeth-Jane Burnett, *The Grassling*

Kate Brown, *Manual for Survival: A Chernobyl Guide to the Future*

Roderick Beaton, *Greece: Biography of a Modern Nation*

Matt Parker, *Humble Pi: A Comedy of Maths Errors*

Ruchir Sharma, *Democracy on the Road*

David Wallace-Wells, *The Uninhabitable Earth: A Story of the Future*

Randolph M. Nesse, *Good Reasons for Bad Feelings: Insights from the Frontier of Evolutionary Psychiatry*

Anand Giridharadas, *Winners Take All: The Elite Charade of Changing the World*

Richard Bassett, *Last Days in Old Europe: Triste '79, Vienna '85, Prague '89*

Paul Davies, *The Demon in the Machine: How Hidden Webs of Information Are Finally Solving the Mystery of Life*

Toby Green, *A Fistful of Shells: West Africa from the Rise of the Slave Trade to the Age of Revolution*

Paul Dolan, *Happy Ever After: Escaping the Myth of The Perfect Life*

Sunil Amrith, *Unruly Waters: How Mountain Rivers and Monsoons Have Shaped South Asia's History*

Christopher Harding, *Japan Story: In Search of a Nation, 1850 to the Present*

Timothy Day, *I Saw Eternity the Other Night: King's College, Cambridge, and an English Singing Style*

Richard Abels, *Aethelred the Unready: The Failed King*

Eric Kaufmann, *Whiteshift: Populism, Immigration and the Future of White Majorities*

Alan Greenspan and Adrian Wooldridge, *Capitalism in America: A History*

Philip Hensher, *The Penguin Book of the Contemporary British Short Story*

Paul Collier, *The Future of Capitalism: Facing the New Anxieties*

Andrew Roberts, *Churchill: Walking With Destiny*

Tim Flannery, *Europe: A Natural History*

T. M. Devine, *The Scottish Clearances: A History of the Dispossessed, 1600-1900*

Robert Plomin, *Blueprint: How DNA Makes Us Who We Are*

Michael Lewis, *The Fifth Risk: Undoing Democracy*

Diarmaid MacCulloch, *Thomas Cromwell: A Life*

Ramachandra Guha, *Gandhi: 1914-1948*

Slavoj Žižek, *Like a Thief in Broad Daylight: Power in the Era of Post-Humanity*

Neil MacGregor, *Living with the Gods: On Beliefs and Peoples*

Peter Biskind, *The Sky is Falling: How Vampires, Zombies, Androids and Superheroes Made America Great for Extremism*

Robert Skidelsky, *Money and Government: A Challenge to Mainstream Economics*

Helen Parr, *Our Boys: The Story of a Paratrooper*

David Gilmour, *The British in India: Three Centuries of Ambition and Experience*

Jonathan Haidt and Greg Lukianoff, *The Coddling of the American Mind: How Good Intentions and Bad Ideas are Setting up a Generation for Failure*

Ian Kershaw, *Roller-Coaster: Europe, 1950-2017*

Adam Tooze, *Crashed: How a Decade of Financial Crises Changed the World*

Edmund King, *Henry I: The Father of His People*

Lilia M. Schwarcz and Heloisa M. Starling, *Brazil: A Biography*

Jesse Norman, *Adam Smith: What He Thought, and Why it Matters*

Philip Augur, *The Bank that Lived a Little: Barclays in the Age of the Very Free Market*

Christopher Andrew, *The Secret World: A History of Intelligence*

David Edgerton, *The Rise and Fall of the British Nation: A Twentieth-Century History*

Julian Jackson, *A Certain Idea of France: The Life of Charles de Gaulle*

Owen Hatherley, *Trans-Europe Express*

Richard Wilkinson and Kate Pickett, *The Inner Level: How More Equal Societies Reduce Stress, Restore Sanity and Improve Everyone's Wellbeing*

Paul Kildea, *Chopin's Piano: A Journey Through Romanticism*

Seymour M. Hersh, *Reporter: A Memoir*

Michael Pollan, *How to Change Your Mind: The New Science of Psychedelics*

David Christian, *Origin Story: A Big History of Everything*

Judea Pearl and Dana Mackenzie, *The Book of Why: The New Science of Cause and Effect*

David Graeber, *Bullshit Jobs: A Theory*

Serhii Plokhy, *Chernobyl: History of a Tragedy*

Michael McFaul, *From Cold War to Hot Peace: The Inside Story of Russia and America*

Paul Broks, *The Darker the Night, the Brighter the Stars: A Neuropsychologist's Odyssey*

Lawrence Wright, *God Save Texas: A Journey into the Future of America*

John Gray, *Seven Types of Atheism*

Carlo Rovelli, *The Order of Time*

Mariana Mazzucato, *The Value of Everything: Making and Taking in the Global Economy*

Richard Vinen, *The Long '68: Radical Protest and Its Enemies*

Kishore Mahbubani, *Has the West Lost It?: A Provocation*

John Lewis Gaddis, *On Grand Strategy*

Richard Overy, *The Birth of the RAF, 1918: The World's First Air Force*

Francis Pryor, *Paths to the Past: Encounters with Britain's Hidden Landscapes*

Helen Castor, *Elizabeth I: A Study in Insecurity*

Ken Robinson and Lou Aronica, *You, Your Child and School*

Leonard Mlodinow, *Elastic: Flexible Thinking in a Constantly Changing World*

Nick Chater, *The Mind is Flat: The Illusion of Mental Depth and The Improvised Mind*

Michio Kaku, *The Future of Humanity: Terraforming Mars, Interstellar Travel, Immortality, and Our Destiny Beyond*

Thomas Asbridge, *Richard I: The Crusader King*

Richard Sennett, *Building and Dwelling: Ethics for the City*

Nassim Nicholas Taleb, *Skin in the Game: Hidden Asymmetries in Daily Life*

Steven Pinker, *Enlightenment Now: The Case for Reason, Science, Humanism and Progress*

Steve Coll, *Directorate S: The C.I.A. and America's Secret Wars in Afghanistan, 2001 - 2006*

Jordan B. Peterson, *12 Rules for Life: An Antidote to Chaos*

Bruno Maçães, *The Dawn of Eurasia: On the Trail of the New World Order*

Brock Bastian, *The Other Side of Happiness: Embracing a More Fearless Approach to Living*

Ryan Lavelle, *Cnut: The North Sea King*

Tim Blanning, *George I: The Lucky King*

Thomas Cogswell, *James I: The Phoenix King*

Pete Souza, *Obama, An Intimate Portrait: The Historic Presidency in Photographs*

Robert Dallek, *Franklin D. Roosevelt: A Political Life*

Norman Davies, *Beneath Another Sky: A Global Journey into History*

Ian Black, *Enemies and Neighbours: Arabs and Jews in Palestine and Israel, 1917-2017*

Martin Goodman, *A History of Judaism*

Shami Chakrabarti, *Of Women: In the 21st Century*

Stephen Kotkin, *Stalin, Vol. II: Waiting for Hitler, 1928-1941*